T0196431

Creating Opportunities at the Edge of Chaos

Edward Mutema

WESTBOW®
PRESS
A DIVISION OF THOMAS NELSON
& ZONDERVAN

WestBow Press books may be ordered through booksellers or by contacting:

WestBow Press
A Division of Thomas Nelson & Zondervan
1663 Liberty Drive
Bloomington, IN 47403
www.westbowpress.com
1 (866) 928-1240

ISBN: 978-1-4908-5926-2 (sc)
ISBN: 978-1-4908-5927-9 (hc)
ISBN: 978-1-4908-5925-5 (e)

Library of Congress Control Number: 2014919910

Printed in the United States of America.

WestBow Press rev. date: 12/5/2014

Contents

Dedication

This book is dedicated to my late mother Elizabeth. A tireless woman of prayer who prayed me into the Kingdom of God but went to heaven too soon before she could welcome her daughter in law and her grand children. And also to my late father Freddie, who had great faith in me.

Acknowledgements

I would like to thank my lovely wife, Tererai, and my wonderful children, Bongai, Gareth and Janice for their prayerful support and encouragement, and for holding me accountable as I wrote this book.

To my friends and prayer partners, Nick and Debbie Griffiths, Isaac and Evelyn Dodd.

To my friends Chad and Faith Gandiya, Ngoni and Loriat Sengwe, Dzengo and Faith Mzengeza, who have travelled with me on this journey from the beginning.

To all those behind the scene including Onias Tapera, who urged me to write.

To God be the glory.

Author's Confession

This book has taken a long time to write for two reasons. It was overtaken by clutter, the maze of things least important that surfaced along the way. Partly as a result came a resurgence of procrastination – the thief of investment, thanks to the failure to prioritise.

I now complete this book recognizing my weaknesses. My lack of urgency is ironic in itself: I succumbed to sheer indiscipline and lack of focus, key messages that the book was intended to convey in its original form.

What still remains the focus of this book is that at any time God can use what we have to create what we do not have. There is never a time we should give up because it has too soon become too late and impossible.

I am excited that at last you can read the blossomed nuggets, thoughts, and ideas that I hope will take you to another level. We are all works in progress. The time this writing has taken produced a deep vein of experiences, bitter and sweet. I am that much wiser, with more understanding and discernment, and hope this book will be a source of reflection on the mightier matters of life.

May you be able to create opportunities out of the potentially explosive circumstances along your journey. That remains my prayer, hope, and belief. Enjoy!

Create

Yes create. You have the potential, and God made you that way. There is never a dull moment when you realize the purpose for your being on planet Earth.

Jesus walked on mother Earth for thirty-something years, culminating in three years of vision-driven leadership "to seek and save the lost". Each day was packed, action-oriented. And the job was done when he cried, "It is finished!" on Easter Friday.

Never a dull moment. Challenges? Yes. We live at the edge, every day. We run up against life-changing situations, broken families, political upheaval – even natural disasters, tsunamis and the lot.

Welcome to our world. It encompasses hope for the hopeless, nuggets of gold within a heap of useless rubble. God is still in the business of picking up the broken pieces of our lives and creating opportunities at the edge of chaos.

Take heart. You have great potential: to create out of nothing, to see what others don't see, to sing a song that others can't sing – to dream, to change, to live comfortably at the edge.

As you read through these pages, may you reflect on you, on Jesus, and on the heroes of faith – all those who were able within their lifetime to achieve greatness by overcoming obstacles at the edge of chaos.

So start now. Create.

The Leader in You

Leadership is all to do with creating opportunities. You are never in the comfort zone. It is all to do with creativity and innovation. Leadership is all to do with hope and determination. You cannot afford to entertain defeat and pessimism. You cannot afford to mull over the negative all the time.

Leadership is all to do with painting a vision of the future and the tools for achieving it. It has nothing to do with mere dreams without the passion to sustain those dreams. The focus is always on success, and failure is only conceived as the other end of success.

Leadership has to do with vulnerability, the recognition that we all have a darker self. Leadership has to do with serving others when emotionally that may not be the right thing to do.

Leaders are men and women of all seasons. They both determine their own weather and let others do it for them. Leaders take charge at the same time as they allow others to lead them for the common good.

Jesus is our model of leadership. He lived at the edge of chaos, always. At Nazareth he was taken to the edge of the precipice. He walked away and was soon preaching and performing miracles in the next town. He revolutionised the world at the edge of chaos.

He preached with authority. His message was transformational. For the three years of his ministry, it was not business as usual. He ruffled the feathers of the kingdom of Satan. He used the power of the written Word to resist principalities and powers. His battleground was sometimes within the synagogue. And the religious leaders became his greatest critics. His opposition was within the religious establishment. He was under constant surveillance. Yet this strengthened his resolve to complete his assignment and to regard the enemy as an opportunity.

You lead with confidence. You lead in faith. You exercise care about what you call impossible. You seek to create something from nothing so as to achieve your objective, and you cause things to happen.

Leaders will always make a difference. They discern the difference too. You see further than others can see. You arrive at the destination before others do. You tap from God's reservoir before others do.

This is why Solomon asked God for wisdom. He could discern the difference between right and wrong. This discernment enabled him to live by God's principles and to shun corruption. He could resist the pressure to please, to compromise, and to cut corners. These are vital ingredients for wise leadership in today's world.

Wise leaders are focused on where they are going. Everything else is an obstacle to be overcome in order to achieve the objectives. Wise leaders are selfless. They are like the heroes and heroines of the faith in the Book of Hebrews. "What a record all these have won by their faith! Yet they did not receive what God had promised, because God had decided on an even better plan for us" (Heb. 11: 39–40, GNT).

You have no reason for despondency. Don't despair; only hope and trust.

This is the paradox of leadership. You die in order to live. You suffer in order to enjoy life. You lose in order to gain. You are despised, and yet you are honoured. You are poor, and yet you are rich. This was what Jesus demonstrated. This was his perception of leadership. What a standard to uphold for today's leadership, setting the example of a paradigm shift.

Leaders lift the spirits of followers when the chips are down. Jesus did. Leaders find a way when there seems to be a cul-de-sac. Jesus did. Leaders consider crises as opportunities. Jesus did. And leaders have a bag full of positives and far fewer negatives.

It is clear that leaders need a sustainable resource base in order to sustain them. Jesus's resource was God. He never did anything on his own. He relied on the Father. He paid the ultimate sacrifice: death on a cross.

The heroes of the faith had constant communication with God. They depended on him. And so the modern leader has to do the same. This will ensure that even at the edge of chaos, it will still be possible to lead.

This is leadership par excellence. Let chaos and crises help create opportunities. This way we will be emulating the King of Kings and the Lord of Lords.

Making a difference in my life and in other people's lives is hard work. You can never be the same. You will lose in order to gain. You may die in order to live. Something has to give way. This is the way of leadership. This is the way Jesus led the band of twelve into the greatest life-giving, life-changing movement of all time. It was transformational. It was passion-driven and spoke to the hearts of men and women. It was strategy based, resource connected, and focused on meeting the needs of people. Failure was not an option, as the driving force was the King of Kings and the Lord of Lords.

We make a difference when we keep connected to the source. Jesus urged his followers to shine. He declared, "I am the light of the world." Because he was the light, those who responded to his teaching would reflect that light too. Stay connected, and exude light. Stay connected, and lead the way Jesus did.

If you want to be a moral disinfectant, be the salt of the earth. Salt makes a difference. In our morally depraved world, we can only live differently if we are connected to a holy and righteous God. We can only understand what love is if we emulate him. "We love because he first loved us" (1 John 4: 19). We can understand love between husband and wife only if we follow the example of Jesus, who sacrificed his life for the sake of the church.

Jesus is the change agent. A relationship with him has made the church triumph over odds today and in centuries past. Peter and John, when confronted by religious authorities who wanted to put them in jail, demonstrated the importance of this connectedness in their famous statement: "We must obey God rather than men" (Acts 5: 29). Those present were astonished because these men were not educated; their only qualification was that they had been with Jesus. Wow!

The basis for triumph, for victory in this challenging world, remains relational. We are told, "And Jesus increased in wisdom and in stature and in favor with God and man" (Luke 2: 52). When he reached thirty and began his three-year ministry, the result was dynamism, passion and influence. He too was connected to the very end: "Then Jesus, calling out with a loud voice, said, 'Father, into your hands I commit my spirit!' And having said this he breathed his last" (Luke 23: 46).

Our first priority as we seek to make a difference is to ensure we stay connected. If we do, it will be far easier to turn crises into opportunities.

"By the Rivers of Babylon": Hope in Despair

Going into exile for the Jews was tragic. A once-revered, chosen nation suffered the humility of servitude for a season. David captures the sombre mood of the people of God this way: "By the rivers of Babylon we sat and wept when we remembered Zion" (Ps. 137: 1, NIV) They were asked to sing the songs of Zion, but they could not. It was a depressing time.

Babylon felt like the road to nowhere. All hope had been lost, leaving only for God's promise. Imagine leading a people in such a predicament. Prophets were in a league of their own, telling it as it was, striking a cadence of faith and hope for a people disillusioned by their circumstance. What a task! This is the essence of leadership: creating hope where there is none, inspiring when hearts are sinking, pointing the way through chaos.

Yet God's promises stood the test of time. Many lost hope, but God's remnant remained. In time, Babylon was no more. A new day, a new era came into being. Today the Jewish nation remains intact – evidence of God's faithfulness. "For all the promises of God find their Yes in him. That is why it is through him that we utter our Amen to God for his glory" (2 Cor. 1: 20).

You can experience periods of exile. As a leader you may have times when you are lonely and distraught, with few friends and little support. Jesus felt it in the Garden of Gethsemane. Deserted by his inner circle, he was agonising, traumatised, and vulnerable. His help came from above. "And there appeared to him an angel from heaven, strengthening him" (Luke 22: 43). He did not buckle or succumb. He stood the test at a time of crisis.

You are not alone. In the exile of your life, Babylon may look foreign. Your leadership position may be lonely at the top. Hang on! It is for a purpose. What God has promised will surely come to pass. What is important is to look for the opportunities, to resist pessimism, to fight lethargy, and to avoid self-fulfilling prophecies. You may say to yourself: "Oh, this is fate. There is nothing I can do. This is the end for me. No one ever came out of such a situation as this." Wrong. Daniel came out of the den of lions. Joseph came out of prison to become prince. Paul and Silas prayed and sang their way out of prison. And the list is endless.

In Babylon, the Jews were asked to sing the Lord's song. How could they, when they were in such trying times? When you know you are in God's will, you can sing. Circumstances cannot dictate your mood. They cannot set your agenda. You do. Your future is not based on emotions but on God's promises. Your strategy wrapped in God's strategy will triumph.

Lead Where Your Heart Is

Doing what you love is natural. It breeds excitement, passion. It is from the guts, not from the head. When you release your talent, your adrenaline kicks in. And you do it. Not prompted, but willingly.

Jesus said, "For where your treasure is, there your heart will be also" (Matt. 6: 21). Your gift or talent is your investment. Utilise it. It will help you create opportunities.

It is still hard work. You still exercise discipline. But you lead better and act better when you do what you love doing.

Unfortunately, many don't. Many engineers and teachers, for example, who find themselves out of a job in a foreign land, do what they have no passion for in the Diaspora. They wake up in the morning sad to go to work. Their only driving force is cash: they have to feed families. It is survival.

Identify what you do best. Something that gets you excited when you do it unsolicited. Do it. Practice it. Pray about it. Re-skill yourself.

God has promised to establish the work of your hands. " You shall eat the fruit of the labor of your hands; you shall be blessed, and it shall be well with you"(Psalm 128:2). And King Solomon says, "Whatever your hand finds to do, do it with your might, for there is no work or thought or knowledge or wisdom in Sheol, to which you are going" (Eccles. 9: 10).

Paul the apostle exemplified this. He was so passionate about people that he said, "For I could wish that I myself were accursed and cut off from Christ for the sake of my brothers, my kinsmen according to the flesh" (Rom. 9: 3). He was so dedicated to the Christian cause that, in his farewell address to the Ephesian elders, he said, "But I don't care what happens to me, as long as I finish the work that the Lord Jesus gave me to do. And that work is to tell the good news about God's great kindness" (Acts 20: 24,

CEV). He had sleepless nights talking and preaching. He was consumed by his passion.

Today many people find no satisfaction in what they do. Performance is low. You have to push them in order to motivate them. It is hard. You hear people say, "I am bored stiff at work." These are telltale signs of a demotivated person. What a contrast to Paul's philosophy, "Give thanks in all circumstances; for this is the will of God in Christ Jesus for you" (1 Thess. 5: 18). Where your heart is, there is a driving passion that keeps you keeping on. There is an inner joy and fulfilment that what you are doing comes from the gut and not the head. You set a very high standard for yourself, God's standard. And when the job is done, there is satisfaction. And I have done this with all my heart.

The result is that you impact positively those whom you interact with. If you are a teacher, such an attitude is infectious. It catches on. And soon there is a buzz of excitement. When you lead where your heart is, you can never be the same again. Neither can those you are in contact with.

Imagine Jesus as he taught during his day. Crowds gathered, drawn to remain with him. The stories he told and the way he told them mesmerised them. No wonder the religious leaders were impressed about Jesus, "for he was teaching them as one who had authority, and not as their scribes" (Matt. 7: 29).

Multi-skilled leadership is no longer an option. The world demands leaders who can make informed and discerning choices:

- Leaders who show compassion like Jesus did.
- Assertive leaders with the passion of Paul.
- Determined leaders with the resolve of Daniel in Babylon.
- Vulnerable leaders with the humility of David, who are willing to acknowledge their darker self just as did Paul, who admitted, "The saying is trustworthy and deserving of full acceptance, that Christ Jesus came into the world to save sinners, of whom I am the foremost" (1 Tim. 1: 15).
- Vision-driven leaders who see further than others see, like the great heroes of the faith.

Lead where your heart is. To the migrant who finds himself in a foreign land, this becomes a challenge. For example, the engineer who cannot find a job must lead in the moment. They adjust, adapt and pray that the love of Christ will bring passion to their adopted career. There is need to change peoples' mindset today as they are now called to do jobs that they never intended to do. There is need for accepting that we can serve God sometimes through a career that we did not originally choose.

This phenomenon is global in extent and may be the greatest challenge Christians are facing as a result of globalization. You need to find God in the context that he puts you in. God wants you to remain focused on him wherever you are, whether in the comfort zone or on the precipice. The bottom line for the Christian is to find out whether God is living and moving in your plans.

Paul, speaking of Jesus, cried out, "that I may know him and the power of his resurrection, and may share his sufferings, becoming like him in his death" (Phil. 3: 10). All else was history – in fact, rubbish. His preoccupation was to ensure that he was living in accordance with God's will. The acid test for leadership that satisfies the soul is to realize that one is doing what God wants and at least have peace with God. For Paul, even prison was where God's will was to be executed. The powerful epistles he wrote from prison demonstrate what God can do despite our circumstances. Ordinarily any author would look for a serene environment, away from any bustle or stress, to pen important documents. Not according to God's mysterious plans. This is a clear illustration of our complete dependence on God, wherever we are. We can exercise our talents wherever God places us. The important thing is to respond to the challenges in God's way.

Jesus's Model

Jesus is the person who made the ultimate difference even when the chips were down. Servanthood became an asset in his ministry. God recognized Jesus and exalted him above every other name.

Jesus showed respect. He demonstrated peace to his enemies and in the end won the whole world. "He committed no sin, neither was deceit found in his mouth" (1 Pet. 2: 22). What a contrast to some of today's leaders. Many try to weaken the influence of their subordinates, in their absence. They seek to receive glory at the expense of others. Christian organizations suffer from this all the time. In the end you get praise singers and few honest and open colleagues who seek to make their organization a witness to others.

Insults were hurled at Jesus, but he never retaliated. He was made to suffer but made no threats. This is leadership par excellence. Jesus refused to use his power and influence to change the course of God's plan for his life. He instead decided to remain an example for generations to follow.

You may be struggling to retain composure and peace when people deride you or simply provoke you for no good reason. It is not by asserting your position that you will win others but by the calm spirit of reflection and love. This was the hallmark of Jesus' character. This will ensure that those you lead and those under your influence will forever glorify your Father who is in heaven.

This is not a sign of weakness. I am not suggesting that you cannot state your position clearly. But the key is how you do it. You should not "bruise the peaches". When you attack people's character and self-esteem, you lose them. And it may be difficult to restore them to take their place and become involved in the organization. You can attack their role but must not hurt their self-esteem.

This is why Jesus was always at the cutting edge of making a difference to those he encountered. It didn't matter whether it was a woman caught in adultery, a tax collector hated by the Jews, a man possessed by a demon, or the ever-talking Peter. He remained consistent. He loved people more than things. He was indeed the Great Shepherd of the sheep. We should emulate him as we seek to lead others on his behalf in whatever context.

Who Is Fooling Whom?

God examines your motives. This is leadership from within. God needs to know the leader within before he can be impressed by the leader without. Christian leadership is all about leading in both the realm of the visible and the invisible.

What is your motivation? Jeremiah says, "Has this house, which is called by my name, become a den of robbers in your eyes? Behold, I myself have seen it, declares the LORD" (Jer. 7: 11). In other words, who is fooling whom? Whom are you impressing? Are you accountable to someone greater than your immediate environment?

God searches the heart. He cannot be fooled. And when something is done for him, the standard is high. It is all about excellence. This is why it is a tough assignment. It is all about watching and praying and not sleeping and resting as did the most favoured of Jesus's disciples in Gethsemane.

Some of the greatest challenges facing leaders today are the pressure to please, the pressure to compromise, and the pressure to tolerate. It is therefore important to search one's motives and refrain from pretending or playing to the gallery. Those in politics, especially in some parts of Africa, will know that it is extremely difficult to be oneself and to speak the truth.

The greatest challenge is to compromise, to go with the flow and never seek to challenge. This is now common in some Christian organizations that are autocratic in nature. In order to protect one's position, one will outwardly agree with the leadership while inwardly harbouring grave sentiments of disapproval. There is hidden underneath the *me* that people think I am and not the *me* that I really am. Why can't people be free to honestly serve God? Why such bondage?

The Pharisees were masters at this sort of deception. But, as Jesus said, "Woe to you, scribes and Pharisees, hypocrites! For you shut the kingdom of heaven in people's faces. For you neither enter yourselves nor allow those who would enter to go in" (Matt. 23: 13). There are leaders who for years prevent others from attaining their full potential by the manner in which they demonstrate their leadership style. People are put off positions of responsibility because the leader cannot take off the lid of suppression, threat, fear, and downright hypocrisy.

Jesus had nothing to hide. He was open. He was criticized, and yet he never sinned. He allowed it. He created an environment where people were free to air their views and to express their humanity without fear.

Leading at the edge of chaos requires that we come out of our comfort zone and into the realm of the impossible. Leadership becomes an enterprise of risking all to achieve God's objectives. Paul insisted on doing God's will even when the Holy Spirit had revealed to him the obstacles that he was likely to face along the way. Now that is vision-driven leadership: a passion for the cause that drowns the waves of defeat and negativity, a clear vision of what to do, how to do it, and when – a zeal coupled with a dogged determination to accomplish the task.

Paul was so consumed by his mission that he saw nothing else but that mission. It didn't matter whether he encountered turmoil in the world. The psalmist adopts a similar attitude:

God is our refuge and strength,
a very present help in trouble.
Therefore we will not fear though the earth gives way,
though the mountains be moved into the heart of the sea,
though its waters roar and foam,
though the mountains tremble at its swelling. *Selah*.
(Ps. 46: 1–3)

Can one lead in a chaotic environment? Yes, but only if God is at the centre of that leadership. Can one lead in a politically volatile environment? Yes, but again, only if Jesus is at the centre of one's mission. David did, so did Daniel, Deborah, Nehemiah, Paul. Can one lead a family in turmoil? Yes.

Jesus was always on the edge of chaos, but he created opportunities. He never mourned over the state of things in his environment but sought to improve the situation for the better. Many of us cry over spilt milk, and our period of mourning as leaders becomes a stumbling block as we fail to see other doors that God is prepared to open. One of the greatest tragedies in Africa is people thinking about past failures instead of going forward to deal with the present and the future. The unlocking of talents and gifts is slowed down when people mourn over their past failures instead of "taking up their mats" and moving on. Leaders move on, and failure is not an option. Time and tide wait for no one; so it is with our leadership. Too much analysis of the chaos may hinder or slow down the problem-solving potential we have.

Every chaotic environment produces nuggets: ideas, plans, opportunities, paradigms and an aggressive approach to problem solving. So seize it!

The Power of Letting Go

The story of Ruth is a clear example of someone, Naomi, who exercised the power of letting go. She gave her daughters-in-law a choice to either remain with her or to leave and get on with their lives. She realized that leaving would empower them to realize God's call and purpose in their lives.

Letting go is one of the most difficult things to do. You feel a loss. There is a feeling of "it will never be the same again". And yet this is a sign of great leadership. It is empowerment. It is recognition that you are dependent on God who created all things and that all our lives are in God's hands.

When our children were young, we never thought we would see a time when they would leave home and be independent from us. When that time comes, it is traumatic, it is a mourning period. We feel a sense of loss. We are not sure whether they will be able to take care of themselves, even though over the years we have been preparing them for this new life. We feel insecure without them and find it difficult to remain the two of us without their company.

What a feeling the disciples must have had when Jesus was taken away from them in a cloud. They must have been shattered. Their world ended with a bang. He was no longer with them. The one they had always relied on, when storms broke and when demons threatened, was gone. But Jesus had empowered them. He had promised to be with them until the end of the world. Still, that was not enough. They wanted his physical presence.

What a relief when the Holy Spirit came upon them after days of waiting in prayer. Jesus's words were fulfilled: "But you will receive power when the Holy Spirit has come upon you, and you will be my witnesses in Jerusalem and in all Judea and Samaria, and to the end of the earth" (Acts 1: 8). At last they were released like doves, free to soar and do his will. They were afraid no more. They were able now to confront the enemy.

Notice that all this anxiety, the inability to let go, was a problem to the disciples and not to Jesus. At one point they reported to Jesus that they had found someone doing what Jesus did and wanted to stop him. And they were envious. Jesus quickly gave them a lesson that positive competition was acceptable as long as the goal was the same. "For the one who is not against us is for us" (Mark 9: 40).

He was satisfied that he had prepared the ground for them to assume responsibility in a hostile environment. He assured them in John's Gospel, "I have said these things to you, that in me you may have peace. In the world you will have tribulation. But take heart; I have overcome the world" (John 16: 33). When you have done your work as a leader and you are secure in what you have prepared in advance for your followers, you can leave and rest and enjoy seeing the fruit of your labour.

Jesus was a perfect example. After three years of teaching, training, and coaching, it was finished – job done, and he was "out of here!" Now we are waiting for the next phase, his second coming. Leadership doesn't get better than that. You can learn lessons. You can let go because your work is done. You can let go because God can do the rest. The bottom line is knowing the purpose in your life's journey. Jesus knew and stuck to it. Why don't we?

The Art of Waiting

Waiting is strategic. While you wait, you equip yourself. You position yourself. You anticipate what might happen. You prevent the fire. You are proactive. The children of Israel waited 430 years in Egypt. God was preparing Moses. Jethro was being prepared to be Moses' father-in-law, in the desert!

While you wait, you scout around for opportunities. While you wait, you equip yourself.

We are living in an impatient environment. Things should have been done yesterday. We are on the move all the time. Isaiah prophesied about this thousands of years ago, when he said, "They who wait for the LORD shall renew their strength; they shall mount up with wings like eagles; they shall run and not be weary; they shall walk and not faint" (Isa. 40: 31). He gives the picture of an eagle. An eagle at thirty goes through a renewal process, so it can live for another thirty years. Waiting is renewal time. You reflect. You strategize. You go back to the drawing board. You revisit the vision. You gather strength to be ready for liftoff!

Paul in Galatians (see 5: 22–23) regards patience as a fruit of the Spirit. The eagle is skilled in waiting before it pounces on its prey. So does the lion and any other predator. When the time had fully come, Jesus was born (see Gal. 4: 4). Notice, *when the time had fully come*. It meant waiting for the right time.

We have talked about strategic positioning before, the need to be at the right place at the right time. This is a conscious and deliberate strategy. Its goal is that when the right time comes, one just seizes the opportunity and is ready to roll.

You need to be vigilant. You wait in expectation. You can't afford to wait aimlessly, without focus. Time will pass you by, and you will achieve little. In Jerusalem the band of followers of Jesus became prayer warriors in waiting. They were in the upper room praying expectantly. They were spiritual lookouts!

You don't mourn. You pray. You read, training and teaching yourself. You become a Scout. You prepare yourself.

Life is a waiting game. While we wait, we are born, we live, and ultimately we die. And while we wait, we should be responsible, accountable, and productive. Everything is in preparation for the big day when we say adios to the world – and hello to a new life, if we have prepared for it. So you cannot afford to slack off or rest on your laurels. It's essential to take initiative and be proactive. In order to create opportunities at the edge of chaos you must be prepared to wait before exploiting opportunities.

Be an Example

Leadership is not just an art; it is a way of life. Remember that "Jesus increased in wisdom and in stature and in favor with God and man" (Luke 2: 52). He lived a character that drew the attention of God.

While leaders may impress outside the home, the people who really know them are their immediate family, their spouse and children. Pharisees, on the other hand, were masters at deception. They were hypocritical. They did not lead by example.

Today, this is the acid test. Are you a role model? Or are you a cover-up? Jesus led by example. Paul said, "Be imitators of me, as I am of Christ" (1 Cor. 11: 1). It is all about transparency and accountability. This is where one needs to impress – daily; in season and out of season.

You are in the spotlight, every day. Jesus was. Paul was. So was Joseph in Potiphar's house, when she tried to blackmail him. And his response? "He is not greater in this house than I am, nor has he kept back anything from me except you, because you are his wife. How then can I do this great wickedness and sin against God?" (Gen. 39: 9). This is the key. You are not doing it for yourself. You are doing it for God. You have a reputation to uphold. For some, a corporate reputation is at stake. But for others, it is all about Jesus.

A father does not fool around and expect his children to become saints. A director will not compromise and look to his subordinates for ethical living. A national leader cannot "preach" about sacrifice and yet at the same time live luxuriously at the expense of the population. Jesus once remarked, "Foxes have holes, but the son of Man does not have anywhere to lay his head." That is exampling! A good shepherd lays down his life for the sake of the sheep. He is selfless. He thinks of others. He desires the good in others. He gets a kick out of doing good, always. If you want to create opportunities at the edge of chaos, be an example.

Be a Person for All Seasons

Habakkuk sums up what our attitude should be as we seek to serve God at all times:

> Though the fig tree should not blossom,
> nor fruit be on the vines,
> the produce of the olive fail
> and the fields yield no food,
> the flock be cut off from the fold
> and there be no herd in the stalls,
> yet I will rejoice in the LORD;
> I WILL TAKE JOY IN THE GOD OF MY SALVATION.
> (HAB. 3: 17–18).

This should be the bottom-line, always. This has been the mindset of people in the Scriptures that God used. This is what it takes to be a leader in today's volatile world, whether a husband, a teacher, or a CEO. God is at the epicenter. Be resolutely dependent on the One who created all and overcame all obstacles. It is all about consistency, about holding on. Persistence is the key, not intelligence. The world is full of derelict geniuses. God wants us to be consistent, not to be as fickle as the weather.

When you cannot seem to withstand the rigors of life or to understand why God allows certain tragedies to come your way, you are not alone. Elijah the prophet nearly committed suicide when he thought he was the only prophet left. Jonah wanted to take his own life. And Moses had almost given up on God.

But this was Jesus's response in the Garden of Gethsemane: "My Father, if it be possible, let this cup pass from me; nevertheless, not as I will, but as you will" (Matt. 26: 39). These are words coming out of a traumatic experience, from the desperation that comes when you are tested to the limit and in danger of losing your grip. You can hear the words "Hold on!" and yet you have no stamina left. You are squeezed to the last drop. You are about to throw in the towel. Friends seem to disappear; in Jesus's case, they were fast asleep, unperturbed, and yawning their life away!

David did experience this many times over when Saul, the spiritless king, pursued him on every front. It was through this experience that he came out singing in Ps. 23: 5 (CEB), "You set a table for me right in front of my enemies." That is the correct attitude, in season and out of season.

> Even though I walk through the valley of the shadow of death,
> I will fear no evil,
> for you are with me;
> your rod and your staff,
> they comfort me. (Ps. 23: 4)

God remains God. His love endures forever.

> Opportunity often comes disguised in the form of misfortune or temporary defeat.
> —Napoleon Hill

You may experience animosity within your family as an errant child, with people speaking evil of you. Nothing seems to go your way. But God is with you. As Paul writes, "If God is for us, who can be against us?" (see Romans 8:31). Yes, this God – the Creator, the great I Am, the beginning and the end, the All-Present, All-Knowing, All-Loving God. If he is alongside you, supporting you, he is all you need to create opportunities at the edge of chaos. God will take care of you.

Paul, being taken to Rome by sea, went through a devastating storm. The ship was about to sink. Everyone aboard had lost hope. An angel reassured Paul: "This very night there stood before me an angel of the God to whom I belong and whom I worship, and he said, 'Do not be afraid, Paul; you must stand before Caesar. And behold, God has granted you all those who sail with you'" (Acts 27: 23–24). What an assurance. You could be on the verge, on the precipice. Take heart. God is in the driving seat. Relax. The turbulence will soon be over.

And writing to the people of Rome, Paul the great philosopher says: "What then shall we say to these things? If God is for us, who can be against us?" (Rom. 8: 31) How profound! God, the Creator of the universe, the Almighty, who is everywhere present, all-knowing, God who is so big and yet so loving, who through Jesus came to seek and to save the lost ... Paul says, if he is on our side, who dares mess with us? If God is for us, surely "who dares wins!" Such is our confidence that, even at the edge of chaos, each of us can say, with the psalmist, that "I will fear no evil, for you are with me".

Just as trees battle it out during the winter months, bare, stripped, and seemingly without life, so can we. Paul experienced this in his travels. And his response: "We are often troubled, but not crushed; sometimes in doubt, but never in despair; there are many enemies, but we are never without a friend, though badly hurt at times, we are not destroyed." The secret: "At all times we carry in our mortal bodies the death of Jesus, so that his life also may be seen in our bodies."

God is with you "until the end of the age" – in season and out of season. When you battle with crises at home, in the workplace, in your marriage, in the family, he is there. When you fail to manage yourself or suffer from a debilitating disease, he is there. His grace is sufficient.

When you are leading in recession and out of recession, it's like the marriage vows: "for richer, for poorer, in sickness and in health". You create love where there is none. You experience joy where there is despondency. You laugh, you smile, you encourage. You manifest the fruit of the Holy Spirit: love, joy, peace, goodness, gentleness, and the rest.

You are consistent. It's not easy, and yet it's worth it. What a difference from what happens around you every day. People are frantic. They swear, they curse. They have not a moment to spare, endlessly impatient. What a contrast!

Opportunities abound in and out of season. On the edge. On the precipice.

Lead by Faith and Not by Sight

This is what makes leaders tick. This is what should make you tick. They see what others don't see, dream what others don't dream. They lead in expectation. They lead by faith, not by sight. They strategize, plan, take risks, and execute, with God's help.

King Solomon, the wisest man of his time, realized this: "We may make our plans, but God has the last word" (see Prov. 19: 21). Behind every great leader is a greater God. We must acknowledge that when we ask the Lord to bless our plans, He will ensure that they are successful.. This is true faith.

Paul, one of the most successful leaders in Christendom, walked by faith. His reasons? "I have been crucified with Christ. It is no longer I who live, but Christ who lives in me. And the life that I live in the flesh I live by faith in the Son of God, who loved me and gave himself for me" (Gal. 2: 20). What tremendous words. What a resume!

Because I have done away with self, I am no longer living the life that I want but am led by Christ himself, because he lives in me. Here are the implications: because he lives in me, there is a change in the way I see things. And because he lives in me, I am transformed by the renewal of my mind. Because he lives in me, I no longer do my will, but the will of him who sent me. Because he lives in me, nothing can separate me from the love of God which is in Christ Jesus. Because he lives in me, my decisions on marriage, relationships, and a career are all subject to the scrutiny of him who called me. Because he lives in me, my battles our won through the Spirit, for "'Not by might nor by power but by my Spirit,' says the LORD of hosts" (Zech. 4: 6). Because he lives in me, my tolerance of others who are not necessarily my type is transformed by the One who lives in me. Because he lives in me, I walk not by sight but by faith, just as he walked.

I no longer see things in the natural but in the spiritual. I no longer believe through seeing but through faith, through the knowledge that God is in control, and all that he desires will come to fruition. As Habakkuk put it, "the just shall live by faith" (2: 4). I am dependent on God to such an extent that I fear not, for I know that he is with me and that what he has purposed in my life will come to fruition.

When Simon Peter had gone the whole night without catching fish, Jesus told him to put into the deep. And he obliged because Jesus had said so. It is not that Simon had seen fish coming through the nets in droves, but by faith he realized that Jesus, who was the creator of fish, could intervene on his behalf. He had faith in Jesus. Jesus's mother at Cana in Galilee, told the organizers, "do whatever he tells you" (John 2: 5), and the result was the best wine ever tasted at a wedding party!

Because Christ now lives in us, because he has taken over command of us, and because we are now the temple of the Holy Spirit where the Godhead dwells day in and day out, we cannot live in any other way except by faith. This is the way heaven and earth came into existence. Abraham was considered the friend of God through exercising faith when he offered his son Isaac in obedience to God's command.

Creating opportunities can only be done by those who live by faith, because Christ lives in them. We don't need to worry about tomorrow, about clothes, about food, about our very lives. Why? Because Christ who lives in us stirs faith within us. We become dependent on him, and we cast our burdens on him, for he cares about us. When we seek first the kingdom of God and his righteousness, we realize that God knows our needs, and he will take care of all that we need. As we work hard daily God will increase favour on us and ensure that we succeed.

And because Christ lives in us, we should not be anxious about anything because he who dwells in us "knows our needs". He is conscious of what we are facing in life. All he urges us to do is to "seek first the kingdom of God and his righteousness, and all these things will be added unto you" (see Matt. 6: 33). So living by faith means surrendering our marriage, our teenage daughter, our challenging husband to Christ. Why? He is involved because he is part of us. We dare not leave him out of the discussions. He is the solution. This means, "casting all your anxieties on him, because he cares for you" (1 Pet. 5: 7).

And because Christ lives in us, we are like Mephibosheth, who, through David's favour, ate with the king for the rest of his life. The Godhead dwells in us, and this should impact our lives and influence our actions, desires, and behaviours. Paul worked very hard to earn a living. He ended up saying he who does not work should not eat. We become more diligent, show integrity, and care less about our image than our Christian brand, which flows out of our daily experience with Christ. Jesus said, "Whoever does not take his cross and follow me is not worthy of me" (Matt. 10: 38). There is a cost.

This song sums it up:

Because he lives, I can face tomorrow,
Because he lives all fear is gone.
Because he lives I know he holds the future,
And life is worth the living, just because he lives.
   —Bill Gaither

And because he lives in us, it can never be business as usual. When the Godhead decides to resides in us and make our bodies a habitation, we can never be the same.

When Christ lives in us, we yearn with Paul to know Christ and the power of his resurrection. It is through his power that we are able to walk by faith and experience his victory in all that we do.

What God says always comes to be. The Old Testament prophecies were fulfilled with precision, meaning that when the Word says it is no longer I that live but Christ who lives in me, it means just that. When it says that the life that we live in the flesh we live by faith, it means just that.

That gives Christian leaders an extra edge, placing them a cut above mundane figureheads. Your motivation, inspiration, and courage are birthed in the supernatural. Your responses to crises are modelled by the great spiritual giants ranging from Abraham to Jesus. You count the cost, you take risks, you absorb criticism, and you soldier on. You see the end from the beginning. You stay the course, fight the good fight, and finish the race. Wow!

Favour Brings Undeserved Opportunities

The crowd preferred to release Barabbas and not Jesus. In an instant he was free. Little is known about the reaction of Barabbas to this extraordinary turn of events in his life. He was meant for the gallows, but Jesus instead stood in the gap. He was a criminal, but someone took his guilt upon himself in order to set Barabbas free. Here was an undeserved opportunity – a grace opportunity.

There is always a temptation to think that we can strategize our way into opportunities. We easily think it is because of our power and might that we accomplish our goals. No. Our God can do it. The thief on the cross was transformed from criminal to a citizen of Paradise in an instant. All he did was recognize who Jesus was when he said, "Jesus, remember me when you come into your kingdom" (Luke 23: 42). God can turn difficult situations in order to make his name known to all people.

The Bible is awash with stories of men and women who yesterday were despised but suddenly swam in God's love, mercy, and blessing. The key is to realize who we are in Christ and what he can do for us, not what we can do for him. When we obey him, he has promised to intervene appropriately, turn crises into opportunities, and help us create opportunities at the edge of chaos.

It is God's unmerited favour that has lifted the poor from the bottom of the heap to eat with princes. Jesus told a story of workers who were employed at different times for the same wage. At the end of the day when the employer was paying up, those who came early complained that they were receiving the same amount as those who had been contracted at the end of the day.

For these workers, fairness meant that they had to be treated better because they were at it earlier than the others. They wanted to be put into a different league from the other group. In other words, they were better than others, and they wanted to be treated so. They did not want to be lumped with these other lazy workers who came later and still wanted to be given the same amount.

But the response of the employer was rather revealing. He had agreed on a wage separately with different workers. He had not reneged on the agreement. So for those who came earlier to complain of unfairness was not fair. God will treat everyone the same so long as they have a relationship with him. His grace is sufficient for everyone. He is not influenced by the way we look at others. He doesn't discriminate but treats everyone the same as long as they are in a covenant relationship with him.

There is lots of emphasis today on performance management, our ability to be great achievers. While this is commendable for the achievement of organizational objectives, Jesus in this story shows that we are finally at the mercy of him who called us in the first place. The Bible says that "God shows his love for us in that while we were still sinners, Christ died for us" (Rom. 5: 8). It was not when we were doing fine, excelling, but at our lowest ebb. It was his grace, initiated by him that brought us to himself.

We have to realize that opportunities sometimes come to us not through our own power but through God. Think of the life of Joseph. As a boy, little did he realize that God would bring him to Egypt. But somehow, through a serious of events, God brought him through adversity and suffering to his destiny. Unmerited favour operating in his life led to his success story.

Moses was rescued from the river Nile and exiled as a fugitive. On his way to ending up in Pharaoh's palace, surely he never thought he would be leading the greatest nation on earth after spending forty years in the desert. All this was through the grace of God. He could not argue that he deserved it.

This is the paradigm shift Jesus taught his disciples. This is the story of salvation. The initiative comes from God, and he uses whatever skills we have to fulfil his purposes. There are many stories of men and women whose destiny looks cut off, but suddenly, out of nowhere, the tables are turned, and God works out his plan.

> The trouble with opportunity is that it always comes disguised as hard work.
>
> —Herbert V. Prochnow

That is why it is possible to create opportunities at the edge of chaos. Favour plays a crucial part in our turnaround strategies. The key is to keep hoping, Stay focused. Live right. Keep emulating Jesus as your role model.

His mission was simple: to seek and to save the lost. He never wavered. And within three years, it was mission accomplished. Today the impact of that mission is felt across the world; in art, music, dance, architecture, and transformed lives – a world living in hope.

When others struggle and cannot understand what is happening around them, you rely on God and ask him to intervene in these situations.

You Are the Special One

Many times favour is all you need. You cannot explain it. Some call it a breakthrough. You are desperate for a job. Suddenly you meet someone who connects you to someone who can offer their services. You happen to mention your particular project at a dinner. Interest is generated, and you close a deal there and then.

Barabbas, the reputed murderer, was in prison during the crucifixion of Jesus. Pilate decided to free Barabbas and not Jesus. Can you imagine what his family must have said to him when he showed up? "How come you are free?", they must have said. Barabbas had no idea why he was free. All he knew was that he was meant for the gallows, but an innocent man took his place. That is favour. Wow!

It is important to be rational. But you need more than pragmatism. Jesus came full of grace. He is the epitome of favour. When you embrace him, you invite favour to determine your destiny. It does not make you a zombie; you plan, execute, and follow up, but all this is wrapped in his grace. This helps you to remain humble, dependent on the creator of resources, who enables you to achieve your vision and goals.

Do you think Barabbas in his right mind would boast that he was able to unshackle himself? Would the blind man boast that he was now able to see? Grace keeps you in check. Paul sums it up: "But by the grace of God I am what I am" (1 Cor. 15: 10). The rest is history.

Grace is the supernatural intervening in the affairs of men and women and completely transforming the task at hand. Grace gives the wow factor to your assignment. It begs a testimony because of the way God demonstrates his power in your leadership, work, and family.

Ezekiel's prophecy captures God's grace in its entirety. God reminds Ezekiel to tell the children of Israel how God raised them from the depths of despair when he found Israel wallowing in their blood with their umbilical cord wrapped round their body. Then, despite having been rescued by God, Israel went on to sin against God. But what is striking is that God told Ezekiel to tell the children that he still loved them and that he would love for them to return to him. In chapter 16: 60 God says through Ezekiel, "Yet I will remember my covenant with you in the days of your youth, and I will establish for you an everlasting covenant."

This is the God who sees us through the crisis. He knows we are vulnerable and that we have not been up to it in our lives, but he still loves us. Sometimes we struggle to forgive, and yet we have been forgiven. We struggle to reconcile, yet Jesus reconciled us back to God. We are impatient, when he has patiently seen us through tough times.

Don't forget! You are bought with a price. You don't own yourself. God is in charge. He is the Provider, the Enabler. Each passing day should be punctuated with gratefulness as we realize and acknowledge the goodness of God. "I can do all things through him who strengthens me" (Phil. 4: 13). All things. Overcome challenges, resolve conflicts, manage errant staff, and the list goes on. Oh, and overcome my weaknesses.!

Be Humble

Be real. Be yourself. No faking. It's back to the basics of being the one God intended you to become. Not condescending but treating others as you would want to be treated. This is true servanthood, genuine and unassuming. It is not temporary but permanent, a whole way of life.

And our example is Christ – meek and lowly, yet exalted and powerful, that "at the name of Jesus every knee should bow ... and every tongue confess that Jesus Christ is Lord, to the glory of God the Father" (Phil. 2: 10–11). That is what humility is all about.

You are humble when you acknowledge who you are before God – insignificant but unique, ordinary but worthy in God's sight. You acknowledge your dependence on God. With such a spirit, you can never brag or get puffed up. This means that should you boast, you can only boast of what God has done for you.

Humility is an asset. It is part of our arsenal in spiritual warfare. It is the secret that unleashes God's ability to use us. Repeat this to yourself, "Humble yourselves before the Lord, and he will exalt you" (Jas. 4: 10). Humility disables the enemy, who does not realize that when we are weak, that is when we are strong.

This has been the hallmark of men and women of God throughout the ages. Leaders who are humble know when to go. They recognize that others are better than themselves. They listen. They are patient. They don't glory in themselves. Remember Stephen, Paul, Hannah, David, Jeremiah, and the Lord Jesus, who, though he was God, "did not count equality with God, a thing to be grasped, but emptied himself, by taking the form of a servant" (Phil. 2: 6–7). It is in our moment of weakness, when we are exposed and shamed in front of others, that God's power is demonstrated. Even when Jesus hung on that cross of shame together with criminals, being derided by many in broad daylight, still the purposes of God were being worked out. And the centurion could still remark, "Truly this was the Son of God" (Matt. 27: 54).

Through the humiliation still shines the radiant truth that God is in it and will triumph. The greatest prophecies in the Old Testament were against nations that God used, but instead of humbling themselves before God, they became proud at heart; hence their demise. Even the nation of Israel, chosen against all odds by God himself, became proud and arrogant, leading to God's severe punishment on his people.

The Bible says, "Vengeance is mine, I will repay, says the Lord" (Rom. 12: 19). It is not for us to worry about those who seek to bring us down, who seek to expose our weaknesses in public for the sake of momentary acclaim and self-gratification. Let them. All we can hold on to is his word, which tells us that if we humble ourselves before the Lord, he will lift us up. What he requires of us is acknowledging him even when the chips are down and leaving the rest to him.

Remember how David was humiliated by Saul. He was made to run into the wilderness and seek refuge in the darkest of places. And yet he remained humble. He would not raise a finger against "God's anointed," as he referred to Saul.

Don't Be Afraid

Fear has been the devil's weapon from the time he was driven out of heaven. The writer to the Hebrews says that Jesus came to deal with the fear of death (2: 15). When you are afraid, you can't take risks. When you are afraid, you lose confidence. When you are afraid, you doubt. Fear hesitates but faith jumps at the earliest opportunity. And John says, "There is no fear in love, but perfect love drives out fear. For fear has to do with punishment, and whoever fears has not been perfected in love" (1 John 4: 8).

Fear sees not opportunities but danger. All it cares about is running away from the situation. In both the Old and New Testaments, God urges people not to fear. On many occasions, people failed to realize who God was and how his presence meant that there was no need to fear. David says, "Even though I walk through the valley of the shadow of death, I will fear no evil, for you are with me" (Ps. 23: 4).

Jesus says, "Fear not, therefore; you are of more value than many sparrows" (Matt. 10: 31). The person Jesus told us to fear was the one who had the power to put both body and soul into hell. And that is God himself. So none else qualifies to be feared except God

When you fear, you doubt God. You are subconsciously saying that he is not really in control. This is why God says that without faith, it is impossible to please him (Heb. 11: 6). Faith is the opposite of fear. Either we have faith, or we fear. We cannot have the two together. In fact, if we say we love God, we will have faith in him and therefore have no fear.

This has been a real struggle for me, especially when I am struck down by illness. The tendency is to lose hope and to think of the worst in my situation. But one day, God reminded me through his word that it was faith, not fear, that would sustain me.

Jesus said to Peter, "You of little faith, why did you doubt?" (Matt. 14: 31). When Peter decided to follow Jesus on the water, he started well, looking to Jesus, but suddenly he looked at the wind and then he began to sink. He took his focus off the Father of faith and doubted the one who had asked him to walk on water. We cannot create opportunities if we have doubts. We cannot create opportunities if we lose our focus.

The book of James talks about wisdom and how to receive it. You can only receive it in faith – that is, if you don't doubt. And we cannot survive without wisdom, and yet it is only by faith that God can give it to us.

Jesus was a man with a mission. He was a man who depended on his Father. At his baptism the confirmation came: "And behold, a voice from heaven said, 'This is my beloved Son, with whom I am well pleased'" (Matt. 3: 17). In the gospels he consistently talks about doing his Father's will. He wanted to do the work that he was sent to do. It is this kind of focus and purpose that can help us through difficult situations and turn such situations into a sea of opportunities. Are you prepared to unlock that potential? Then do not be afraid. Only believe. Depend on God.

The devil has always preyed on our fear. In fact this is one of the reasons Jesus came, to deal with such fear. In Hebrews, it says, "Since therefore the children share in flesh and blood, he himself likewise partook of the same things, that through death he might destroy the one who has the power of death, that is, the devil and deliver all those who through fear of death were subject to lifelong slavery" (Heb. 2: 14–15).

Notice that Satan preys on the fear of death. While people are aware that they are going to die at some point, it is the fear of death that may hasten that predicament. And Jesus came to destroy the one who brought about that fear. We are therefore freed from that fear, and we need to claim that promise and not fear.

You cannot create opportunities or make a difference if you are afraid all the time. We are more than conquerors, a victorious people, not because of ourselves but because of what God has done for us. In African traditional religion the fear of death is still being used to make people lose hope, fearing to take risks and generally feeling powerless in the face of adversity.

Faith, unlike fear, jumps at the earliest possible opportunity.

Faith holds on to the promises of God and is fully dependent on God. When Jesus said to Simon Peter, "Throw into the deep," after he had been fishing the whole night without catching fish, Peter seized the opportunity and did what Jesus had told him. Surely Peter, an experienced fisherman, could have decided not to believe what Jesus said. This was an act of courage. He did not consider the negative consequences of his action.

You know what happens when our faith is tinted with doubt. We always say, "What if it doesn't happen?" When we believe, we put all our eggs in one basket. We stake everything on what God says.

When we gave our lives to Christ, it was an act of faith. Imagine always thinking, *What if Jesus has not saved me?* This would be detrimental to our faith, and it would not yield the results God intended. Sometimes when you are out of a job, there is a tendency to think that you will never get a job. But the Scriptures say, "If you ask me anything in my name, I will do it" (John 14: 14)

You are unique. There is no copy of you in the whole world. Ours is a lifestyle that is governed by whom we believe. We live by his principles. Since the global economic crisis, the language of the kingdom has become currency. Honesty, integrity, morality, and sincerity are now common vocabulary branded on mass media. The world of business, politics, and governance has begun to realize the importance of living in accordance with the demands of a kingdom lifestyle.

As Paul quoted one of the ancient poets, "In Him we live and move and have our being" (Acts 17: 28). We live not in a vacuum but in God. We are not on our own. We are dependent on him. And his principles govern how we live and move. We need his wisdom in order to operate effectively in this world.

Acknowledge God

God is the power behind your leadership. He is your Father. There is intimacy. There is fellowship. There is camaraderie. It is personal. He becomes your source of strength.

In whatever challenge you face, you exude confidence because of who is for you. Paul summed it up when he said, "If God is for us, who can be against us?" (Rom. 8: 31). It is a declaration you make when confronted with the challenges of life. He becomes your main focus. No weapon formed against you can prosper, because he is the Almighty. He remains in charge of the universe. Under him every knee shall bow, and every tongue shall confess that Jesus is Lord.

He is the beginning and the end. He has a helicopter view of our circumstances, our situations, and our world. He lets us peep into the future if only we will allow him to. He is the Provider; he is our Shepherd. In fact the earth is the Lord's and all that is within it. Talk about strategy, he has it, for this is how he fashioned the world. There is no credit crunch in his vocabulary, for "silver and gold are his".

He is the Creator. He has made us in his image. He is the source of our creative energies. The potential to create out of nothing is rooted in him. He is our Father. In his hands he's got the whole wide world.

Sad that some have got rid of his name. He is no longer acknowledged. No wonder we are in such a mess.

When we make mistakes, he restores us to our original position as soon as we confess our sins. We don't have to be supermen and superwomen. He knows we are but dust.

You Are God's Masterpiece

Embrace your identity. Be proud of it. And exude it always. You will stand tall among others. You will go through life with unrivalled, unmatched confidence. In business, at home, at school wherever you are, your talents and gifts will be exercised without fear. With no inferiority complex, you are willing to face challenges head on.

Defining who we are in Christ will affect what we are in the world and how we react to the many challenges that face us.

Creation out of nothing. God saw opportunities for a universe crafted out of the void. He crafted a masterpiece. He restored our original position through Jesus's death on the cross, and therefore we are special.

Our relationship with Christ brings with it new ways of thinking about ourselves. When Adam and Eve disobeyed God, their original status was destroyed. They lost the right to a special relationship with God. Remember, before this they were on speaking terms with God. They had access to anything. They were in charge of it all, except the tree of the knowledge of good and evil. They were always in the presence of God. And in the presence of God there is safety, security, and abundance. In the presence of God there is no fear.

Faith is a way of life. You communicate with him at will. In the presence of God you are totally dependent on him. He is your reference point. He acts as your advocate in times of crisis. So for Adam and Eve and for us, this is the place to be, always. Moses declared, "If your presence will not go with me, do not bring us up from here" (Ex. 33: 15). God promised Moses that his presence would go with him. Once Adam and Eve were removed from God's presence, they lost their effectiveness. They were unable to face the challenges of life.

You can only lead at the edge of chaos if God's presence is there. Why? Paul sums it up: because God "is able to do far more abundantly than all that we ask for or think, according to the power at work within us" (Eph. 3: 20). A child in the presence of his father can do anything without fear. He will appear confident to challenge other children who may want to tease him. He is peaceful, comfortable, and confident. It is the presence of the father that makes a difference.

You should envision the King of kings as present in your trouble – when the going gets tough and difficult decisions are required. He is there when your soul cries out, replying, "Fear not, I am with you." See him create opportunities at the edge of chaos. Shut your eyes, and don't listen to naysayers. Focus on the task and on what God can do. And "beyond the sky" will be the limit!

Adam and Eve lost their identity when they sinned against God. They were ashamed. Their-self esteem was affected. And it took God some time before that could be restored in Jesus Christ. However, even when they lost this original status, God loved the world so much that he gave his only Son, Jesus. He restored our relationship with the Father. Our uniqueness was restored.

You are wonderfully made. You are special. And you are crafted by the Creator himself. You need not suffer from an inferiority complex. You are who you are not by human workmanship but by God's grace. Each one of us should be defined by what we are in Christ and not by what those around us say to us.

The real you is a brand-new creation from the Father, who does his things in a way that can never be compared to anything in this world. There's no putting a price tag on you. You are priceless. You were made a little lower that the angels. That is why the psalmist says, "What is man that you are mindful of him, and the son of man that you care for him?" (Ps. 8: 4).

Knowledge of who we are in Christ will affect what we think of ourselves and the world around us. We can only boost our self image when we realize what Christ says we are in him. We are priceless. Our citizenship is in heaven. You are blessed with the blessings in heavenly places. You were chosen before the beginning of the world" Wow, that is awesome! The Bible refers to everyone in Christ whether they are rich, poor, disabled, old, young, dumb, lonely. As long as they are in Christ, they are special. In fact whatever God created is special. Remember, each time after God created something, the Bible says, "it was excellent".

Our attitude to what is happening to us, be it political, economic, social should be interpreted on the premise that there is God who has created this world and created us uniquely. The question should always be what opportunities are there in any situation for God to reveal himself. What opportunities are there for us to make a difference from our unique position as Christians, who are special, masterpieces of God? Occasionally one reads in the newspapers of antiques which are later sold for thousands of dollars but which were bought for very little because none realised how precious these items were.

It is only upon close scrutiny by the experts that one realizes how special these items are. God is the specialist who knows how precious we are. People may not realize how special we are but that doesn't matter because ultimately we are responsible to our Maker. You are special, I am special. You are God's Masterpiece, I am God's Masterpiece. We, the masterpieces shall see Jesus as he is. Now, this means that ours is an elevated position. You cannot see the King of Kings if you are not royalty yourself. We are priests of God and we are destined to meet him in the end.

So whatever we face, whatever difficulties we go through, we are special. And all we should see are opportunities. Ours is a life of hope for our God is a God of hope. Ours is a life of faith for God is the Author and Finisher of our faith. Ours is a life of endurance, for He endured the cross, despising its shame. So whatever people say or think. Remember who you are in Christ first.

Confidence in who you are becomes a launching pad for effective leadership in the kingdom of God. You exert influence. You are willing to take risks. You become proactive. You can take challenges head on knowing that you are unique. You believe in yourself. People tend to believe in someone who exudes with confidence. You are a special one.

Take Risks

Peter and John were fishermen. Then came this walking preacher called Jesus. "Leave what you are doing and follow me. I am offering you a brand new assignment, fishing for men." What? They did leave – and changed the world forever.

These men took risks. Leaving their profession and following someone who they had just met. Successful people always take risks. So did Colonel Sanders, the founder of KFC, who started his dream at age sixty-five! He got a Social Security check for only $105 and was angry. Instead of complaining, though, he did something about it. He thought restaurant owners would love his fried chicken recipe. They would use it, sales would increase, and he'd get a percentage of it. He drove around the country knocking on doors, sleeping in his car, wearing his white suit. Do you know how many times people said no till he got one yes? One thousand and nine times.

John Grisham, the American author, started out as a lawyer who loved to write. His first book *A Time to Kill*, took three years to write. The book was rejected twenty-eight times until he got one yes for a 5,000-copy print run. He's sold over 250 million total copies of his books.

Manage Yourself

It's essential to manage your anger, your lust, your impatience. Otherwise you run riot, out of control.

A fish starts to rot from the head. Don't fool yourself and think it doesn't matter what you do. The *me* that you really are is more important than the *me* that people think you are. Paul in the Bible says that unless you can manage your family, you are not fit to manage others. You may be a corporate executive or a leader of the local village store; regardless, integrity matters. It is the stuff that oils the relationship wheel. And such relationships last. They are sustainable.

You hear of corrupt leaders, pastors, politicians, and academics. No surprises there, because they have failed to manage themselves. They are good out there and not good in there – in their soul. You can start now. It is never too late. When you mess up, you can still stand up and walk again. The future, stupid, not the past. Where you are going matters and not where you have been. Remember, if it is a mis-take, you can take it again!

Wisdom and understanding are the keys to managing oneself. Leaders discern, anticipate, and are intuitive. Jesus grew in wisdom. This is the ability to discern the difference, to see what others don't see. When there seems to be no way out, and the situation looks bleak, the leader in you sees opportunity and a way out. There is no room for pessimism. We live in hope.

You need wisdom and understanding to manage your family. They are another sort of corporate organization. You need a plan, a purpose, and a strategy. Your success within this nucleus arrangement becomes a launching pad for greater success elsewhere.

Many people ignore their families. They become heroes at work and villains at home. They can handle corporate challenges and yet struggle to foster long-lasting relationships with their families. Charity has to begin at home. Your success is measured by the sort of legacy you leave at home. Sadly this is being ignored.

Leaders are glorified for national achievements and vilified for family debacles.

Character is at the heart of proper management of oneself and in turn of others. You lead by example because you are the leader of God's house. The Holy Spirit dwells in you, which means the Godhead is in you. What kind of leader ought you to be then?

Be a Servant

Acknowledge others as better than yourself. See the good in others. Serve with diligence and excellence. Do what you set yourself to do. Servanthood is a great way to inspire others.

Jesus came to seek and to serve the lost. He was the greatest servant of all, and what a following. Servanthood is not a sign of weakness. It is a sign of strength. You empower others. You let go, and you watch change taking place. It transforms the environment. Everyone enjoys serving one another. It is therapeutic. A spirit of togetherness is fostered.

Live on the Edge

Jesus lived on the edge from the cradle to the grave, from Bethlehem to Calvary, daily. When he was born, they sought to kill him. When he was teaching, they plotted against him. Even when he performed miracles, they opposed him to the hilt. At his death, they ensured that his grave remained sealed. Yet he triumphed. He overcame. And he left a legacy. So should you.

Daily we are living on the edge, never sure of what is round the corner, whether a sickness, an accident, or a critical decision. This is the lot of "man born of a woman." You cannot run away from it. All you can do is to anticipate it, proactively plan for it, and be ready. This is living by faith because it makes us rely not on ourselves but on God.

Remember that, when Jesus went to Nazareth, his hometown, people did not believe, and because of their unbelief, the Bible says, he could not do many miracles there. It is here where Jesus was nearly thrown over a precipice by people who did not believe that their local boy could claim such authority and power. This was the beginning of a three-year journey of living on the precipice, on the edge, whatever he did.

The example of Jesus shows us that it is possible to make a difference to our communities even when we don't live from day to day in the comfort zone. Jesus was constantly confronted by hostile religious leaders. He had to fulfil his mission in such an environment. And boy, didn't he do it well! People were spying on him, some sent to make false accusations, and still others challenging his authority, all in the name of religion. No wonder he said that the kingdom of God suffers violence.

Part of what this means is that we need to aggressively seize the kingdom, or rather fight our way through. Ours should be a conscious and deliberate strategy to fight against all principalities and powers. These may manifest themselves through the church, through friends, or through our work environment. Whichever way, as Jesus did, we can still live on the edge and succeed. What a difference it makes to be making a difference for the cause of Christ.

Living on the edge brings new opportunities where you can reach and grasp them. When you step over the edge, you experience new opportunities. The impossible becomes possible. You step away from your comfort zone, willing to confront the challenges of life.

Dealing with opposition from within can be very difficult, whether it's from the church, your own close family, or trusted friends. When they alerted Jesus that his family, including his mother, brothers, and sisters, were outside to see him, he gave a rather untraditional response: "My mother, brothers, and sisters are those who do the will of my Father" (see Matt. 12: 50). Your family is not a comfort. Opposition can come from within. You are still on the edge, and anything can happen. And the thing that helps us survive the challenges of living on the edge is the knowledge that it is not by might nor by power but by God's Spirit.

We need to take the whole armour of God so that we may be able to stand in the evil day. Jesus realized this from the beginning, and he acted accordingly in his hometown. One of the cultural downsides for people, say, in other parts of Africa, is that there is too much emphasis on relationships. This can reach the point that, for some Christian families, compromising one's faith for the sake of family unity becomes a major preoccupation.

People don't want to risk severing relationships, even when it means compromising their faith. Jesus was very clear, bold and adamant. He said on another occasion, "He who loves his father or mother more than me is not my disciple" (to rephrase Luke 14: 26). He was not against loving our parents, but if such love takes precedence over total commitment to Christ, then it becomes idolatry. It is anathema to the things of the Lord.

True relationships are not just biological but spiritual. He proclaimed, "Who are my brothers and sisters, but those who do the will of my Father?" As we commit ourselves to Christ, relationships are transformed into something not transient but permanent. These relationships find fulfillment in Christ when one day, as one big kingdom family, we shall all appear before the judgement seat of Christ. We shall all participate in the final banquet with Christ at the head.

Living at the edge can mean the possibility of losing close relations in pursuit of a greater goal. It is the bigger picture that matters. It is God and his demands. Tough! Can you relate to this? How have you resolved such a dilemma in your life? What are the implications?

Be Joyful

On one glorious afternoon, in a dream, I was taken to a valley where thousands of people clad in white clothes were congregated, and it seemed that the coming of the Lord was at hand. And as I waited, we began to utter these words: "We worship you, Lord Jesus. Come, Lord Jesus." There was a joy unspeakable within us as we waited for his coming. I have never felt such ecstasy, joy, peace, and expectancy, as I couldn't wait to see my Redeemer.

But it was a dream. Isn't this what loving Jesus is all about? Living in hope. Knowing that our citizenship is in heaven, from whence we await a Saviour. We can afford to live at the edge of chaos, because we know that we are only sojourners – not here permanently, but en route to meeting our Lord and Saviour. Our attitude to what happens to us in this world is inspired by what we expect to see in the future.

Leading by Behaviour

The corporate world is desperate for people whose behaviour matches their actions. This is ethical leadership. You cannot divorce your character from what you do and how you do it. Hypocrisy is the opposite of leading by behaviour. Exampling and coaching demand that the leader's behaviour demonstrates integrity, honesty, and faithfulness.

You cannot fake who you are. Sheer intelligence and corporate skills are not enough to persuade others to follow your example. I am reminded of a colleague who would bring girlfriends to hotel rooms. One day, he came to my room and said, "I am not a leader. I mess up all the time when I am away." Interesting observation. For him, leadership was more than just facts and figures. It demanded more from him, from his character.

You cannot fool God. He knows. He sees. He hears. And so do all those around you. Remember the first couple in the Bible? They were transparent. But the moment they disregarded God's instructions, they hid. They were ashamed. They had messed up.

Behaviour defines who we are. It demonstrates what stuff we are made of. It is an outer picture of an inner character. Such is priceless. The world is looking for individuals like this who can "turn the world upside down" for good – forever.

Creating Opportunities for Healing

Perhaps Jesus's greatest act was reconciling the world to God. Sin had created a gulf between God and the human race. There was animosity. The world was dying, and unless something happened, we were all doomed to perish. No wonder Jesus went to hell to sort out relationships there and restore humankind to their original position.

This began a healing process in the midst of a chaotic environment. And Jesus wants us to do likewise. This is why leadership takes a lot out of people. Jesus died in the process. God is in the business of picking up the pieces. We should do the same. You are your brother's keeper. Your attitude should be that of restoring broken relationships, not destroying them – mending, not tearing apart. Be good to everyone.

In what others regard as impossible situations, you are called upon to regard them as opportunities for mending and reconstructing broken relationships. Following a speech on Zimbabwe to a group of donors, one lady came up to me and said, "That is not the normal view that people present about Zimbabwe. You really are Mr Optimistic!"

I had urged Christians to pray positively for the situation, expecting God to intervene. This seems to be what Jesus did when confronted with very difficult situations. While he did not condone certain situations, he made sure that people would experience peace as a result of his intervention. He was always in a reconstructive mode, rather than being destructive, as was the habit of the religious leaders of his day.

There has been a tendency among many Christians to pass the buck and never take responsibility for reconciliation. Many communities are hurting because God has not been able to raise up men and women able to stand in the gap for his people. This demands integrity, commitment, and dedication. When Jesus embarked on the reconciliation process, he ended up on the cross.

I am reminded of my attempt many years ago to reconcile two Christian sisters who were at loggerheads over some relationship issue and had not been able to speak to each other for weeks. As I began the process, one of the sisters was cross with me one afternoon as I was about to attend an afternoon class. She shouted, "Who do you think you are? Are you trying to be holy or something?" I immediately retreated and went straight to my room and cried to the Lord.

After an hour of prayer, a note had been shoved under my door by one of the girls inviting me to go to her room. As I approached the room, to my surprise, I heard people giggling. When I walked in, the two were there and they said, "Thank you for your efforts – we are reconciled!" Years after this incident, I had letters from the two urging me to continue with my ministry of reconciliation. Little did they realize how difficult this had been, with the tears, the anguish, the embarrassment.

Plenty of people will condemn, but few who will restore the broken-hearted. It is easier to destroy than to rebuild. Mother Theresa, Mahatma Gandhi, and Nelson Mandela all played their role in healing a hurting people. They paid the price. The world is a better place, thanks to their efforts. South Africa set up a Truth Commission to heal the wounds. This was Jesus's mission. To heal the broken-hearted. To set free the captives. Are you willing to play such a role at work and in your community?

A Hurting Nation - An Opportunity

Nations are hurting. Between natural disasters, terrorism, dictatorships, and moral decadence, our world is hurting. Although economic prosperity has brought with it material benefits, it is sad to see how it has wreaked havoc on culture, tradition, and the moral fabric of society. While phenomenal growth in the church is being registered from "developing nations", the opposite is happening in "developed nations" with a few exceptions.

The task of healing people remains a major pre-occupation for those who endeavour to create opportunities at the edge of chaos. In varied settings it is the responsibility of Christian leadership to ensure that God's word is heard and heeded. The spiritual decay of a nation is not seen only in political decay but can also be discerned from its lack of "righteousness". Righteousness exalts a nation.

One of the greatest challenges facing so-called affluent nations is the absence of an inner fulfilment that comes from an encounter with God himself. Going into schools is an eye-opener as one comes across children who are not focused, detest authority, and yearn for something that they cannot get hold of. They are bitter and seek to rebel against anyone who comes their way. They are bored. They respond negatively. They have a behaviour problem.

This is a great opportunity for healing. How does one go about rescuing this generation from total demise? The state can't do it, and parents, ill-equipped, are struggling. The generation gap further strains the relationship. Whole families are on the precipice, at the edge. You hear people saying they have fallen out with their dad and mum. They haven't seen them for years. Many mothers languish in nursing homes, cared for by workers with hardly a visit from family. A broken society? Or a hurting one? Who will mend these relationships?

Be the reconciler. Take the initiative. Think of others, not yourself. This may be in response to a family altercation, a misunderstanding at work or a corporate debacle that needs sorting out.

That is what Jesus came to do. We had no relationship with God. Jesus bridged the gap. Now we can be on talking terms with God himself.

We can all become bridges. When people are on the edge in their relationships, we can transform this into an opportunity to build relationships. In tough times, we can soften hearts. In grieving times, people can find solace. In desperate times we can point them to the veteran – Jesus. In his hour of desperation, he cried, "Father, if you are willing, remove this cup from me. Nevertheless, not my will, but yours, be done" (Luke 22: 42). Confronted with an army that wanted to kill him, he was at peace. He could have called ten thousands to defend him, but because he was meek, he controlled his power in order to fulfil his objective: to seek and to save the lost.

Creating Opportunities in an Insecure Environment

September 11, 2001, changed our perception of the world and ushered in a new era of insecurity. It brought home to the ordinary citizen an appreciation of what people in Soweto, Rwanda, Israel, and the West Bank had already experienced over the years. It made people realize how transitory this life is. No guarantees except to hold on to Christ and his promises in the Bible. The sojourner mind set finally dawned. People realized that life is a journey, and its destination is definitely not on this planet. And in the midst of this chaotic situation, people were hurting and they are still hurting. The challenge continues to be for men and women who can help mend broken hearts through God's word. You can make a difference. You can help change the environment, where you are.

Living on the Edge in the Diaspora

Many millions of Africans live in the Diaspora. These are people of African origin living outside the continent where they interact as communities and seek to support their motherland. However, diaspora can also mean the dispersion of any people from their homeland. They have left their countries for political, social, economic, or other reasons. Many of them are Christians eager to serve their Master in a foreign land. Just as the Jews in Babylon did, they face many challenges. A great deal is happening by the rivers of today's Babylon – in the Diaspora. Already some are stuck in difficult situations that have resulted in loss of their loved ones, divorces, and family breakdowns.

Stories from people living in the Diaspora are heart-rending. For some, living for Jesus has become theoretical as they have ended up in situations that require them to lie, cheat, and be devious. People are under pressure to make a living, and in the process, they lose focus on things that matter to God. There is freedom in the air! No scrutiny from anyone. Many find themselves caught up in the things of this world and have very little time for God. Some, whose faith was not as strong when they left their country, end up as lukewarm Christians, having lost the power of faith. Their lives are full of broken relationships, marriage breakdowns child-rearing issues. It's a full-blown identity crisis, a complete reversal of roles.

The story of Daniel and his friends in Babylon illustrates the importance of keeping to the traditions of one's faith in spite of the circumstances. They maintained a lifestyle of prayer and dietary observances, adhering to faith principles even though they were under pressure to do otherwise. They did not succumb to the pressure to please, to compromise, and to cut corners. Most important, they remained principled and resolved in their hearts not to sin against God.

These are the key issues for anyone who finds himself in a

different environment. Daniel and his godly friends could have easily joined in and become like the others, but they didn't. They could have immersed themselves in the idol worship of the Babylonians, but they didn't.

Remember Moses? He grew up in one of the greatest palaces in the world and yet never forgot his roots. He continued to identify with his God and his people. Remember Joseph, who became one of the greatest administrators in ancient Egypt? His fear for God never waned. Remember Nehemiah, serving as a cupbearer in Babylon and hearing of the destruction of Jerusalem? His faith in God was rekindled, and he led his people in the reconstruction of the great city of God, Jerusalem

The Jews in Babylon were asked to sing the Lord's "songs of Zion" in the Diaspora, but they protested, "How can we sing the Lord's song in a foreign land?" This is powerful. People in Babylon, having heard about the history of these slaves from Jerusalem and their track record, wanted them to sing a song. This is one of the most important tests for leadership, for Christians in a completely different environment. God expects you to be in tune with him in spite of your difficulties.

God expects us to rejoice in the Lord always, whatever circumstances we are in. You can sing his praises anywhere, at all times, because you have a relationship with Christ. Joy and peace do not depend on your circumstances but depend on whom you hold on to – especially when the going gets rough.

Jesus was able to say, "Peace, be still," to the winds and the waves because he knew that they were subject to him. And the disciples, forgetting who Jesus was, remarked, "Who is this that even the waves and sea obey him?" Disappointed, Jesus said, "O men of little faith."

The secrets of living in the Diaspora begin with knowing who we are – our identity. We need to live by what God says. Our lifestyle should demonstrate God's character. We are influencers. The moment we lose or demean our identity in a search for acceptability and comfort in our new environment, we begin to compromise, and our influence will be minimal. We definitely won't make the same impact. Peter, writing to the Jews in the Diaspora, was keen to first of all emphasize their status and position, their identity. It was vital that they knew who Jesus was and what he had done for them as the foundation for all they were doing. He then moved on to talk about what manner of life they were expected to live as children of God. And this was not dependent on where they were. God expected them to live in accordance with the manner of their calling, even when facing trials and temptations.

The challenge of family has never been greater. Everywhere today are husbands cheating on their wives, wives cheating on their husbands, and children blatantly defying authority. It is tough living away from "home". The challenge for many in the Diaspora, whether they are English, Chinese, or African, is living a life true to their calling, not a fake existence.

This can be tough. Stories abound of married women and married husbands sharing lodgings as "married" partners. When their bona fide partners then later join them in the Diaspora, they sever these relationships. It all adds up to a life of hypocrisy and intrigue. Some pretend they are not married and get into trouble when the wife turns up at the airport.

Young people face an identity crisis. They find themselves thrust into a cosmopolitan city alone. Parents are hardly at home. They are "shifting" – a crude term for the work-shift pattern. Sitting in front of the latest HD television with unlimited access to the Internet and movies, young people are vulnerable, exposed. The battle of the mind begins. They have no neighbour next door to interact with. Their parents are typically preoccupied with making the most of their time in the Diaspora; where they are sometimes living illegally. They are keen to make the most before the authorities catch up with them and send them home. The old-time religion which they embraced at home slowly becomes entangled in the reality of the now, in the midst of a people who care less for God and more for self and the gratification of their flesh.

Life seems full of contradictions, and they become caught up in the intrigue of rationalisation and sink into an identity crisis. Church becomes a pastime where they go to socialize and to benefit from important contacts who may be willing to chip in when the going gets tough. They attend on the off-chance of securing the odd pound or dollar to make ends meet. This is not fellowship as defined in the Scriptures but fellowship as it meets *my* problems and *my* challenges and ensures *my* reasonable existence in a foreign land.

This is life in the Diaspora. Peter in the Bible used his two letters as manuals of instruction to the Jews in the Diaspora. He reminds them of their context and the skills and competences they need to live a life that is pleasing before God. He interpreted their challenges and difficulties in the light of Jesus, who was treated like a stranger in his own land.

In fact, this is a theme that runs throughout the Scriptures, where the people of God have to have a paradigm shift when it comes to knowing who they are in this world. They are sojourners and always on the move, wherever they are from time to time.

Such a mindset creates a paradigm shift. You think, act, and respond differently. You cannot rest on your laurels. You have to be prepared, alert, and ready to move. You are living at the edge. And you'd better make the most of it.

Hold on at the Edge of Chaos

Chaos is opportunity in disguise. It can be difficult to appreciate when you are on the edge. As we struggle each day, we must hold on as we wait for our Lord to reveal his master plan in our lives. What we consider to be chaos or confusion in our situations now, God may turn into opportunities that we never dreamed of.

Everyone has a story to tell regarding their background, but praise God that he has seen us through difficult times to make us what we are today. I am reminded of my early days when I travelled to the United Kingdom to attend college. I arrived at Heathrow with almost nothing, but God in his wisdom was able to provide for my needs.

Nelson Mandela was an icon. He lived on the edge for twenty-seven years. He became the first black president of a democratic South Africa. Zimbabwe is at the edge of chaos, but we still believe that God has a perfect plan for this beautiful nation.

The God of the night before assures us of his presence and will always be there when we feel uncomfortable in our situations. He knows tomorrow, and he challenges us to stand firm in the faith as we wait for the unfolding of his plans for our lives. We wait in expectation and trust, knowing that God is faithful and he will do as he has planned.

It is important to stay focused on our purpose for being. Too much preoccupation with what might be may cloud our thoughts on what is, what God can do for us today. One of Satan's tactics is to distract us with what might not be, in an attempt to steal our joy about what God is doing in the present. Constant focus on the chaos diverts our attention from the opportunities that God has put along the way.

One preacher said that God wants to appeal to the giant in us and not the grasshopper. When God addressed Gideon as "man of valour", Gideon was taken aback; that was not how he thought of himself. God wants to exploit the great potential in each one of us, and all he requires is our positive response.

As I grew older in my colonial upbringing, I began to realize how much my self-esteem had been affected by situations around me. While I praise God for bringing missionaries to our country, there was a negative side to it. Many people, especially our elderly folk, learned to behave like second-class citizens before the missionary. They could not distinguish between the missionaries and their colonial masters. And missionaries, in accepting this attitude, were not honouring God, who made them in his own image.

Feeling inferior, people were less assertive before the missionary than they should have been. This is not what God intended. We all have the potential to soar as high as possible. We are more than conquerors through Christ who loved us. Creating opportunities at the edge of chaos requires a different mindset. It requires a paradigm shift.

If God is for us, who can be against us? This assurance is crucial if we are going to soldier on despite our circumstances. When we are aligned with God's will, we can go places. Instead of focusing on our present circumstances, we can focus on things that matter.

Like Jesus, we can become reconcilers, breaking down walls of animosity, hate, and greed. Jesus was indeed human, and for thirty-three years he lived on this planet doing what the Father had sent him to do. He broke barriers, he brought peace, and he endured until the end.

The early ministry of Jesus is fascinating. "Jesus increased in wisdom and in stature and in favor with God and man" (Luke 2: 52). This text summarizes his growth and development and teaches us about what he expects of us.

He grew holistically and constantly. His life was dynamic. It did not remain static. He grew in wisdom, one of the most essential qualities of a human being before God. Solomon asked God for wisdom, and God was so impressed with this insightful request that he decided to lavishly shower on him wealth that the world had never seen. The mention of wisdom triggered the whole package that God gives to those who ask.

In fact, it seems that wisdom is the key to unlock every blessing we might think or dream of. This is the very heart of God. In Proverbs it says that creation came about as a result of wisdom. So for Jesus to have wisdom meant he had the same power that God used to create the world.

He had to grow first in wisdom. James says, "If any one lacks wisdom, let him ask God who gives generously to all without reproach and it will be given to him" (Jas. 1: 5). Such wisdom is the ability to discern right from wrong. This is insight. This is seeing before you see. This means anticipation.

Jesus grew in wisdom. He developed in wisdom. He had dynamic understanding of his world and of people. When you read the Gospels, it is clear that how Jesus reacted to the various situations he was confronted with was a clear demonstration of his wisdom.

Even the people remarked that he spoke with authority and not like the scribes. When asked before Pilate whether he was the King of the Jews, Jesus, in a typical wisdom response, remained silent. He was able to discern when to speak and when not to speak, depending on the circumstance and the probable response.

We are living in a world which badly needs this quality. Many of us are respond rashly to our circumstances. We are careless with our lives, not foreseeing the implications of our actions. Many marriages falter because relationships are not governed by understanding the other person's point of view – a hallmark of wisdom.

We are not connected to the source of all wisdom, God. We have disregarded the advice from God our Father and instead let human advice reign supreme. Our children suffer from ignorance of God because we have not exposed them to God's Word and to lives that demonstrate the supremacy of Christ. In other words, we have not been growing in wisdom ourselves, and it is difficult to pass on the baton of wisdom if we are struggling to run the race of wisdom.

When Jesus was left behind by his parents, they found him having a discourse with some of the current religious leaders. Why? Because wisdom is a revelation of God's truths. God reveals himself and makes clear his truths as if you have known them before. So the question was not the age of Jesus, but how much God was prepared to reveal his word through him as a result of the wisdom that he had instilled in him.

When God imparts his wisdom to us, he helps us interpret situations and circumstances differently – through his eyes, not through the eyes of the world. There is always the *aha!* factor when it comes to God's wisdom.

Do you want to create opportunities at the edge of chaos? Ask God, the generous giver of wisdom.

As Jesus increased in wisdom, he also grew physically. Wisdom was housed in a fit and healthy body. It is important to realize the importance of looking after our bodies. Jesus was not an ascetic who neglected his body for the sake of the cause. He was particularly concerned about his physical welfare, knowing that this was God's body, not his.

God wants us to take charge of what he has given us as stewards. And the body is a major part of what God has given us. Paul says "Do you not know that your body is a temple of the Holy Spirit within you, whom you have from God? You are not your own" (1 Cor. 6: 19). We must make sure that it is a fitting abode for the third person of the Trinity. The Godhead should be allowed to dwell in comfort, which comes from a deliberate program to look after it.

This means that our bodies are not a dumping site for garbage in and garbage out. Whatever goes into it should pass through God's quality control to ensure that we don't defile the body itself. We must also determine to ensure that we don't use our bodies inappropriately but carefully and respectfully. There should not be any mutilation of the body as is the practice in some quarters.

In other words, show your body some leadership as you live a life that pleases God.

Jesus's development was not just in wisdom and in stature but in relationships. He grew in favour before both God and people. There is a sense in which this was inevitable. The wisdom Jesus had was a sign of his relationship with the Father. He had a relationship with the Father because the Father had sent him. He did the will of the One who sent him. Jesus would say that he and the Father were one, and at his baptism God demonstrated the kind of relationship he had with Jesus: At the Transfiguration, God says, "This is my beloved Son, with whom I am well pleased; listen to him" (Matt.17: 5). And the centurion at the cross, when he saw Jesus, remarked, "Truly this man was the Son of God" (Mark 15: 39).

One could argue perhaps that Jesus grew in wisdom because he had a relationship with the Father; one might also reason conversely that he had a relationship with the Father because he had the wisdom to realize the importance of having a relationship with the Creator of the universe. A relationship with God comes first if we are to again unlock our potential and see the world as God sees it. Our reaction to what goes on around us should be determined by what kind of relationship we have with God.

Our love for Jesus is judged by what kind of relationship we have with him. Jesus clearly spelt this out when he said that if you love your father and mother more than you love God, you are not fit to be a disciple of Jesus. So a vertical relationship with God is the standard measure for any other relationships we will have. It is a priority. There is no substitute. This comes as a blow to a world which emphasizes *eros* and *phileo* love over love for God. It throws cold water on cultures that deify social relationships at the expense of a love for God. It is when we have God's favour on us that we can effectively carry out God's assignment in the communities where we live.

This is a challenge to many Christian leaders whose desire is to please people instead of consolidating their relationship first. Jesus said, "And you shall love the Lord your God with all your heart and with all your soul and with all your mind and with all your strength" (Mark 12: 30). This was a deliberate commandment that demonstrated the need for first things first. God is our Creator. He loved us before we first loved him. He will be the final arbiter when we stand before the judgment seat of Christ. Our relationship with him is the key that unlocks the doors to his blessings. Jesus had this vital relationship too as he grew as a man.

Naturally following from this, Jesus was in favour with people. He loved people and had a striking relationship with them, always. He was with them in sorrow and in joy. He sought to rescue those whom society looked down upon. He was at the ready to sacrifice his life for others. All this stemmed from the fact that he was full of wisdom and had a close relationship with the Father.

What a life. What a testimony. This is the ideal character that Christ wants to create in us if we are to make a difference in this world. It is not just baseless love for others but a love whose foundation is in God himself. And as God's wisdom flows from us, we are able to deal with people who come to us from diverse backgrounds with diverse needs. We are able to exhibit the same deep sense of compassion that Jesus had. We cannot have this sense of compassion if God's compassion is not in us. And God's compassion can be in us only if we have a relationship with him.

When you get your priorities right, all else becomes a shadow of the real thing. The great martyrs had one thing in common. They were preoccupied with their destiny so much that they considered their present suffering as transitory. Consider Stephen in Acts 7 when faced with a hostile crowd of religious people stoning him. He responded, "Behold, I see the heavens opened, and the Son of Man standing at the right hand of God" (Acts 7: 56). He was operating in a different realm. He was transformed to glory in the midst of a people who thought they had dealt a blow to his faith. He did not allow his circumstances to cloud his vision. He was operating in the heavenly places.

Paul, during his farewell speech to the Ephesian elders again reiterated this mindset. Even when the Holy Spirit had warned him not to go to Jerusalem, he insisted that he had to complete the task that Christ had given him. You see, it is those who press on who will survive at the edge of chaos. Why? Because they are focused, dedicated and committed to the cause. Their passion is to realize God's vision through them and to create opportunities for the gospel of Jesus Christ.

The heroes of the faith listed in Hebrews 11 are all characterized by a determination to keep on keeping on, despite the many difficulties they faced. The majority of them failed to reap the fruit of their labour, but they were satisfied that they had done what they were called to do. Abraham, for example, saw a city he had never been to. This was his motivation. He lived by faith and depended on God for everything.

Passion, Faith, and Perseverance
Pillars of Survival at the Edge of Chaos

When Nehemiah responded to the call to rebuild Jerusalem, it seemed like an impossible task. But God used Nehemiah's vision and skills to create a nation and a city out of nothing. What looked like a chaotic undertaking was shaped through this man's passion for his people, his unbending faith, and his perseverance in the face of vehement opposition.

Nehemiah's personal character and his relationship with God were leadership traits that saw him accomplish great things for God. He was a man of prayer. In fact he sustained himself from God's reservoir. He had unswerving loyalty to the God of Israel and had a great love for the people to whom God had sent him.

To survive spiritually in this chaotic world, we need to strengthen our personal relationship with God and muster enough passion to help us through the trials and temptations of this world. Jesus urged his supporters not to panic, for he had overcome the world. It is important that we see our trials and tribulations, economic downturns, and political upheavals through the eyes of our Maker and interpret them as they really are – transient. This does not mean that we will not feel pain and hurt as we go through it all. But in the midst of it, we can say with Job, "I know that my Redeemer lives, and at the last he will stand upon the earth" (Job 19: 25). It is that certainty amidst confusion and despondency that raises us a cut above the ordinary. It is this faith that helps us sing the Lord's song in adversity.

Daniel, a young man in a foreign land, did not succumb to the temptations and the trials of his day because he had been prepared through the training he received while he was in Israel. He was rooted and grounded in the traditions and strict religious practices of Israel. God was real to him as a teenager, and all else was secondary to him. And even when he was confronted with a difficult choice in the king's palace, he resolved that he would not contaminate himself with food the king offered. Even as a teenager he had moral absolutes – boundaries beyond which he would not go. He resisted the pressure to compromise. His was a lifestyle of prayer, integrity, and faithfulness.

Daniel, like Nehemiah, persevered. If you want to survive at the edge of chaos, you need the spirit of perseverance. Many times we are inclined to give up when the going gets tough. But as Jesus said in the garden of Gethsemane, God's will was paramount, not his. He endured until the end.

It is a matter of holding on to that one believes. The key thing is to be clear about what it is we believe. Paul was clear when he said, "I am not ashamed, for I know whom I have believed, and I am convinced that he is able to guard until that Day what has been entrusted to me" (2 Tim. 1: 12).

We live in a world that makes many demands on us. The Christian life has become a struggle for many as they seek the praise of others instead of seeking God's praise. The contrast between Jesus and the religious leaders of his time, such as the Pharisees, was that they wanted to be seen by others. They wanted to impress. They wanted to show off. The downside of this was that they lost focus on God, so their lives did not reflect the character of God.

There is a growing trend even among Christians today. Many people would prefer recognition from others and not from above. They do not want to show their flawed self, the sinner in them, but pretend to be what they are not. In other words, they are fake. No wonder Jesus talks about God not recognizing what some people did on earth because they were out to please and impress others and not God. Jesus calls these people hypocrites. They pretend to be what they are not.

This breed is found among politicians who behave like chameleons much of the time. In some quarters they are called "rice Christians" because they are in it for what they can get and not for what they can give. Their keenness to please is conditional: as long as they are able to get something. In some countries this is called the "chef mentality" where people will do anything to impress the powerful politician. Sadly, the politician is hoodwinked to think that the followers really like him.

Paul is very clear about this. He tells the Thessalonians how, during the time he was with them, he did not seek to please them but only to please God. The prophets of old were persecuted and even killed for doing just that – pleasing God rather than people. During this time also there were prophets who proclaimed peace or prophesied what the people wanted to hear as a way of pleasing them. God condemned such prophets outright.

It is disheartening now to find, among many of our pastors and rank-and-file Christians, a tendency to conform to worldly standards by becoming who they are not. We are often behaving like Peter in Galatians 2 who, in Paul's absence, entertained the Gentiles but, when he was present, gave the impression he was not for them. No wonder Paul rebuked him to his face.

It's like people who are openly racist when other Christians are not there, but they become inclusive before people whom they respect for fear of being condemned. This is always because people fail to deal with their inner contradictions before God. I have always said there is a hypocrite in all of us. The best way to deal with this is to openly admit our problem and to seek to rectify them through God's help.

If our citizenship is in heaven, we should do all we can not to please our fellow citizens, but ultimately to please him who called us in the first place. It is true that out of fear we sometimes succumb to the temptation to please others as a way to allow the challenge to pass us by without affecting us in any way. The pressure to please is real, and it distracts us from our main goals and mission. We must fight it, or else we will forever remain untrue to ourselves and become inauthentic.

Watch and Pray and Not Sleep and Rest

This is vigilance and patience versus comfort and resignation. The story of Jesus in the garden of Gethsemane is the proper setting for this outstanding lesson in the art of leadership in crisis at the edge of chaos. For Jesus this was the final act of commitment and dedication to his Father before he finally completed the mission for which he had been called by God.

What a way to do it with a group of his select disciples. They were to watch their leader encounter the final struggle before giving up the ghost. He had entrusted them for three years with his power, and here he was performing this final act in their presence.

The episode would unfold over just an hour – not too much to ask of a group of people who had been through thick and thin with Jesus. They had waded through storms and had seen demons being cast out. One of them, Peter, had even walked on water – for a time. And at one time Simon had told Jesus that they had worked all night without catching any fish. Surely waiting for an hour was no big deal, one would have thought!

As Jesus's testing began to unfold and his prayer session intensified, he had to withdraw from the group for a while. It was while he was praying within the hour, that his specially handpicked few dozed off and went off track, forgetting the criticality of the moment. And three times Jesus found them, not discussing what was going on, but sleeping!

God watches over sparrows and also watches over us. David says about God that he never sleeps or slumbers (see Ps. 121: 4). We who are made in his image are expected to do the same. There is so much at stake that we should never lose our concentration but should stay focused. No sentry on duty loses focus lest the enemy should attack unexpectedly. The disciples missed the point. Whether they were tired or not, as Matthew reports, was irrelevant. They were not up to the task, and Jesus admonished them, "Watch and pray that you may not enter into temptation. The spirit indeed is willing, but the flesh is weak" (Matt. 26: 41).

Creating opportunities at the edge of chaos demands vigilance. This means staying alert at all times and concentrating on the core issues that will turn your game plan around. We're challenged to find a dogged determination to accomplish the task in season and out of season and to perseverance even when the odds are against us.

Imagine how disappointed Jesus must have been at his followers. And you too will be disappointed, let down, and abandoned – not by those at a distance but by your close confidants, the very people you put your trust in: your wife, children, and colleagues, your pastor, CEO, or supervisor. Be assured it will happen time and time again. Be encouraged. It happened to the divine- Jesus. He overcame. So will you. He remained focused. So will you.

The key is to go back to the original plan, to the source, to the strategy. Why are you doing what you are doing? Who is the ultimate beneficiary? Foresee the obstacles, and seek solutions. Seek God's will, not your will. And then move on. Your detractors will be left in limbo. You will have transformed your situation from chaos to opportunity.

Get Out of Your Comfort Zone

Peter did, when Jesus asked him to come to him on the water. How daring! It had never been done before – at least not by Peter!

Very often God asks people to get out of their comfort zone. Jonah in the belly of the fish was asked to go to Nineveh. Abraham was asked to leave his people and belongings and head for unknown territory, just like the one-way mission to Mars that is planned for the future. The fishermen were asked to follow Jesus and become "fishers of men," something out of their comfort zone.

All these created opportunities outside their comfort zone. Abraham became father of a nation, Peter became a powerful defender of the gospel, and the disciples changed the world.

Chaos requires us to be vigilant, alert, and innovative. We cannot create or innovate in the comfort zone. Jesus was kept on the run, challenged until the end of his life. One of the greatest challenges facing us today is to prioritize in a world that pressures us to sit back and go with the tide. For Jesus each day was a challenge as he faced opposition from religious leaders. Instead of wallowing in his misery and being pessimistic about the future, he held on to his mission and was determined to fulfil his vision.

When I was a child, on cold winter mornings I would make every excuse to skip going to school. I would prefer lying in bed. But that was short-sighted. I could not become what I wanted to be without the sacrifice, the hard daily slog that goes with it. In the book of Proverbs we are told of ants who labour day and night in order to achieve their goals. The contrast is given by a lazy person who wants "a little slumber".

Jesus led the pack, for in many references in the Gospels we are told that long before dawn he went out to pray. At night he did the same thing. Here was the Son of God, exercising discipline as he sought to create opportunities for the gospel.

You can only get out of your comfort zone if you plan regularly, prioritise wisely, and follow through your plans with a dogged determination. This is the only way to turn a crisis into an opportunity for God. Your focus is not on the crisis but on who can help resolve the crisis. Maintain the core competencies required to address the crisis and a resolve to meet head on the challenges, and watch God move.

And this is not just for a season but always. Life can be likened to a series of mountains. You cannot hop from one to the other. Once on top of one, you have to climb down before you tackle the next one.

The journey is bound to be risky. David summed it up this way: "Even though I walk through the valley of the shadow of death, I will fear no evil, for you are with me" (Ps. 23: 4). The assignment will surely test your resolve. However, in the midst of it all, there is God. There is his presence, the assuring presence of the Creator of the world, who created order out of chaos, the source of ideas, the Mother of invention.

You can get out of your comfort zone into the valley of darkness. You are not alone. Your future is assured. You are strategically positioned to win the battle – God's battle. So what is holding you back? Go on. Leave your comfort zone. And you will create opportunities at the edge of chaos.

Nehemiah did. And he travelled all the way from the comfort of the king's palace in Persia to rebuild a ruined Jerusalem. Armed with God's assurance and the resources pledged by the king, he went. Equipped with prayer and a plan, he tackled the mammoth task of raising the walls of Jerusalem. David, confronted with the mighty army of the Philistines led by Goliath, won the battle single-handed, far from tending sheep in his comfort zone.

You Are God's Mouthpiece

"If you return, I will restore you, and you shall stand before me. If you utter what is precious, and not what is worthless, you shall be as my mouth. They shall turn to you, but you shall not turn to them" (Jer. 15: 19). Jeremiah's prophecy brings out God's expectations of us as we live and move in our world, ready to make an impact on a corrupt people. God says," Therefore thus says the Lord.

You are God's spokesperson. This calls for accountability, responsibility, in the realization that what you say counts. Your response triggers God's response and represents authority and power. So be careful what you say, always.

We can only represent the mouth of God if we usher forth the kind of words that only God can usher – precious words, edifying and encouraging words, words "seasoned with salt", as Paul puts it (see Col. 4: 6). James speaks about the evil that can come from our tongue, which surely can never represent the mouth of God (see Jas. 3: 10–12).

Whenever God has spoken, both in creation and over the years of striving with his people, he has spoken life, abundance, healing, inspiration, and hope. This is the mouth of God. In times of adversity, in crisis at the edge of chaos, this is one of the greatest assets that we need as we interact with people who are without hope, depressed and distraught. We are a cut above everyone as we affect with our mouth the very lives that are devastated and hopeless.

Day to day, as we interact with people at work, at church, and wherever we are, we speak "precious" and not worthless words. What does *precious* mean and how is this a true representation of the God we serve?

God says that people will actually turn to us as we exhibit such character with our mouth. I suppose we will be taking on God's character as our mouth is no longer ours but a true representation of the King of Kings and the Lord of Lords. Have you noticed that those who exude sweetness through their mouth tend to attract and not repel others? There is some fascination about them, wherever they are.

The result is that God will protect and save them. They will be delivered from the enemy. What a comforting thought. As we, through our mouths, represent God by the words that we utter, God will honour that. He will see us through our difficult times, and we will triumph ultimately.

We were created in God's image. We reflect the Creator. We represent him. We are his ambassadors, permanently located on mother earth until we are recalled to be with him, in his kingdom. What you think and say should reflect your relationship with God.

As an ambassador you can only speak as instructed or in accordance with what your Master demands. There is no room for careless talk or for associations with those who have no respect for straight talk. You see, at the edge of chaos, only those who live by the rules survive. They become victorious.

The CVs of People Who Create Opportunities

You cannot transform the world around you if God has not transformed you first. Paul says, "I appeal to you therefore, brothers, by the mercies of God, to present your bodies as a living sacrifice, holy and acceptable to God, which is your spiritual worship. Do not be conformed to this world, but be transformed by the renewal of your mind, that by testing you may discern what is the will of God, what is good and acceptable and perfect" (Rom. 12: 1–2). Those who have given themselves fully to the service of God have the capacity to turn situations around into opportunities. Our relationship with God, specifically how we perceive him and how he perceives us, is crucial in our daily walk with Christ.

This is why Jesus said, "In the same way, let your light shine before others, so that they may see your good works and give glory to your Father who is in heaven" (Matt. 5: 16). When people see your transforming character and glimpse the One you represent on earth, they will appreciate who Jesus is and want to serve him as well. Their experience of our experience becomes therapeutic and will influence others to see their world not negatively but positively.

But it takes men and women of God who have completely surrendered themselves to the Lord for this to happen. Jesus also says, "You are the salt of the earth" (Matt. 5: 13). One of the uses of salt is as a preservative. Instead of the world rotting before our eyes, God uses those of us who have presented their bodies as a living sacrifice to preserve corrupt situations and difficult environments.

You make a difference. It doesn't matter whether everyone else does it, you don't. You are salt. You are not influenced; instead, you influence. Andrew Wommack of Andrew Wommack Ministries on one of his TV broadcasts, *Gospel Truth*, aired on TBN (2014), cited a situation where, during the Vietnam war, he was the only one in a company of two hundred servicemen who did not participate in some of the errant behaviour that went on. He resolved to be salt, to be light. Your curriculum vitae becomes a real-life testimony of who you are, whether alone or in the company of others. You fear God. You are accountable to Him.

Jesus on the cross cried out, "Forgive them, for they do not know what they are doing." This is the hallmark of people who are creators of opportunities. They forgive. They heal. They turn unforgiveness into forgiveness, bitterness into blessing. They transform the environment through their character.

Joseph made one of the most profound statements in Genesis following his reconciliation with his brothers, "As for you, you meant evil against me, but God meant it for good, to bring it about that many people should be kept alive, as they are today" (Gen. 50: 20). Through forgiveness, Joseph was able to turn around an explosive situation in a way that ensured the survival of the Hebrew nation. He created opportunities out of a potentially disastrous situation.

But his character was all important. You cannot turn around situations for good if God has not dealt with you in a manner that makes you ready to be used for his service. In the same way, you cannot look at any situation as beyond salvaging so long you are dependent on the Lord of lords and the King of Kings.

Many of God's people who turned situations around had uncommon humility. Jesus gave the example of a child. This is the very character of Jesus Christ, who, although he was in the form of God, did not count equality with God as a thing to be grasped but he humbled himself and took the form of a servant. The greatest men and women of God have been those who identify themselves with the lowly. And in that process, God turned their situations round. Nehemiah, in his first prayer after the destruction of Jerusalem, identified himself with his people by seeking God's forgiveness for the sins of the nation. Paul, for his part, called himself the chief of sinners. Humility is not a liability but an asset. When you humble yourself, God will put you on a pedestal.

When I took over as head of a certain Christian organization, there was a lady who had been with the organization for over thirty years. While she did not openly resent me, I noticed that she wanted me to realize how experienced she was and how she deserved more respect. Each time I came back from a workshop outside the country, she would complain in meetings that the staff had not been properly briefed. I realized that I needed to swallow my pride with this lady for the sake of winning her. Just before I travelled for a regional meeting, where I was going to spend some days, I called into her office and briefed her on the impending visit, its objectives, and what we hoped to achieve for the organization. Upon my return, I called her personally and briefed her on the workshop and how things had gone on. What a transformation from then on. She was a committed disciple! She felt respected, a true part of the organization, and I'll bet she would have physically come to my defence if the need arose!

When you are humble, you don't overreact. You listen. You anticipate. You allow yourself to be in the shoes of other people with a view to helping them.

Be Tolerant

Here is one of the key characteristics for allowing for sound relationships and the ability to love people. We have to be tolerant. Jesus exercised such tolerance as he came into contact with the lame, the blind, and other social outcasts of his day. This is the ability to sometimes make sure that we regard others as better than ourselves. It is not a weakness but a strength.

In the political world this is very important. Racism and discrimination are perpetrated by people who do not tolerate others but instead regard themselves as holier than others. Hitler went to war over his intolerance of the Jews as an inferior race.

We are all guilty of intolerance, and we need God's forgiveness. At the Council of Jerusalem (see Acts 15), the central issue was the strict Jews who failed to tolerate Christians who were not circumcised, treating them as second-class citizens, contrary to what the word of God says. In fact, Paul rebuked Peter in Galatians 2 for not tolerating the Gentiles and for insisting that he was an apostle to the Jews.

When God appeared to Peter in a vision, he got the message. When he spoke at Cornelius's house, the Spirit was poured out upon the Gentiles as evidence that God was no respecter of persons, contrary to what Peter and the others had thought.

It seems intolerance is everywhere today. People love their inner circle – those who share the same social and religious tastes. They are easier to hang around with, the acceptable, the "normal", the uncontroversial. These are the ones we can easily manipulate.

At the edge of chaos, it is different. There you find all sorts of people – critical, ambivalent, rude, and downright crude. This was Jesus's crowd: a team full of contradictions. And tolerance reigned supreme. The result was peace in the midst of turmoil.

Here is a great lesson for the leader within you. It is easy to accept those whom we love and who fall within our own expectations of race, colour, religion, and creed. In many cases this intolerance is undetectable, embedded in our inner motives, concealed. In truth, we are masters at deception, living in pretence and hypocrisy. Only the Creator sees our motives.

When you are tolerant, you are patient with others. You allow them to grow and mature before your very eyes. You seek to see them be part of you as you embrace them in God's love. First John says that if we hate our brother, it means that we don't love God. How can we love God whom we cannot see if we cannot love our brothers whom we see? The reason we are not tolerant is that we fail to appreciate God's love for us.

Paul says that "the life I now live in the flesh I live by faith in the Son of God, who loved me and gave himself for me" (Gal. 2: 20). He loved us, so you love others. He appreciated you, so you appreciate others. He tolerated you; now you tolerate others. You value others. You have no "attitude" over others. This is the key factor in intolerance, your attitude. And attitude is a habit of thought. You harbour it for days or years, and it manifests itself in your character.

People may not be able to tell you but inside they can feel and sense that the plastic smile is not all about love but is a pretence. You may say, "I don't care." But tolerance should be about accepting the unacceptable. It should be about going the extra mile in embracing those who may not necessarily toe the line and accept us, those we regard as "filthy", impossible, down-and-outs. It is a skill that God gives us. We cannot do this on our own. Jesus has to impart his love to and then through us so we can live a life of tolerance.

When Jesus allowed a woman who lived in sin to wipe her tears from his feet, the disciples were outraged and embarrassed. How could Jesus, the holy God, allow, this to happen in full view of everybody? – associating with a sinner, a woman! They failed to understand the importance of tolerance. We need to exercise it towards everyone, regardless of who they are and what their status is in the community. We are all guilty of this attitude, and we need to repent.

Take church, for example. Someone walks in who is not in the same "league" with you. And you notice and suddenly wish they would not sit next to you. *They may be smelly; I'm not comfortable with these sorts of people*, you think to yourself. You don't say this to anyone.

Eventually they sit next to you. You don't say a word. You wave that old plastic smile in acknowledgement that they are there as a fellow human being, but you would rather they sat somewhere else. You have no choice but to sit out the service, uncomfortable, half thinking about the sermon and half thinking about the person next to you. I have done this before, and I am sure you have. Why? Tolerance is all that's required.

You can create opportunities at the edge of chaos if you exercise tolerance towards those whom you associate with. This has to be a deliberate strategy, genuine, and focused on seeing and accepting people as they are in the eyes of God. It is a prerequisite for team building. It helps your focus as a team. You achieve your goals.

Be Wise

Wise people do create opportunities at the edge of chaos. When you are wise, you are discerning. You have understanding. You are fair and just.

Our greatest model, Jesus, grew in wisdom, and in the love of God and those around him. He lived a balanced life. Wisdom means self-control, diplomacy, understanding, discernment. And God says that he can give this to us generously. One analysis of what has gone wrong with our world is that many of us have failed to utilize God's wisdom. Paul says, "Where is the one who is wise? Where is the scribe? Where is the debater of this age? Has not God made foolish the wisdom of the world?" (1 Cor. 1: 20). It is through the wisdom of God that we can operate our world. When God gave Solomon his wisdom, even the Queen of Sheba, rich and famous as she was, came to marvel at God's gift to Solomon.

Be Wary of Voices

You cannot do God's will if you fail to hear and do what God says. Creation listened to God's voice when he said, "Let there be light." There was light, there was the earth, there was humankind.

When God speaks, we need to hear. When Samuel started off as a young boy serving in the temple under the watchful eye of the veteran priest Eli, he didn't know God's voice. In fact Scripture says that in those days God's voice was not common. And when God called Samuel three times, he went to Eli, thinking he was the one who had called. Samuel was only able to respond to God's voice after Eli told him that it was the Lord calling him and told him how to respond.

In times of crisis, it is imperative to recognize God's voice and respond to it accordingly. In the garden of Gethsemane, Jesus received encouragement from God through the angel who ministered to him. Paul did the same following their shipwreck when he was told to be of good courage.

Jesus summed it up in John 10 when he said, "My sheep hear my voice." Living on the edge, you can't afford to miss his voice.

Concentrate on Issues, Not Tissues

God is all about substance and not trivialities. In fact, "faith is the substance of things hoped for, the evidence of things not seen" (Heb. 11: 1, KJV). In other words, faith is about the "seen unseen"!

This is what should be the flesh of our conversations on a daily basis: talking about things that edify and not destroy. The language of Christians should be about substance and not trivialities. When we fail to focus on the core principles in our lives, we are sidetracked, and we end up in gossip, slander, and the toning down of our passion for God.

Jesus's battle with the religious leaders of his day was to do with their misunderstanding of their purpose in life. They had misconstrued religion and made it petty and frivolous. He urged them at one point to deal with the weightier matters of the law – love, mercy, and justice – and not get bogged down in the traditions and the "add-ups" of the law.

We can only focus on issues if we stick to the things that God says in his word.

Be Expectant

The drive behind successful men and women is that they live in expectation. They are driven by hope. They never allow their circumstances to overshadow their hope for tomorrow. They keep on keeping on. They live in faith and trust and are confident of a better tomorrow.

Countless Christians in situations like Zimbabwe have given up and propagated the gospel of despondency and pessimism instead of positively looking to God for victory. The unfortunate thing about losing expectancy and hope is that you pass the buck. You blame others and not yourself. You refuse to be accountable.

One day I drove by a petrol station to change my car tyre. I began to speak with the receptionist about the problems affecting our country. He said to me that as a Christian, whenever he heard someone criticising the president of the country, he would ask to see the state of their knees. In other words, how much time had they spent praying for those in government and not just criticising them?

He reminded me of my days as a student in the UK when Zimbabwe was still under colonial rule. Stuck on my wall was a large map of the world donated to me by Operation Mobilization. I decided to stick the photos of presidents and prime ministers against their countries so that I could pray for them. When I came to Rhodesia (the future Zimbabwe), I hesitated, as I was now going to pray for Ian Smith who I thought was oppressing my people. But I did post his photo, and from then on, I made a commitment to pray for him as well. It made all the difference to my attitude towards him and all those he represented.

When you pray for someone, it makes a difference. You love them more even if you may disagree with them on certain issues. The parable of the Good Samaritan serves as a good example of how we can overcome our differences as we seek to fulfil one of the most important commandments that the Lord left us.

You can create opportunities only when you look beyond racial, tribal and other differences and seek the common good in other people. The Good Samaritan created an opportunity for service when he turned his enemy into a neighbour by providing him with the resources he needed to carry on with his life.

Without hope, Zimbabwe would never have survived. Christians should be at the forefront of providing that hope. It is true that after 430 years, the people of Israel had almost lost hope and had begun to question the promises of God. But God was faithful in that he continually raised leaders in their midst who helped ignite that hope and in the process bore the brunt of the people's fury and anger.

Gideon, greeted by an angel as "mighty man of valour", had also lost hope and didn't realize the great leadership potential he had. Like the others, he had lost all hope and needed God to remind him of what he could do for his people.

Many of us lie dormant in our churches and in schools whom God would like to raise up for him. Instead of seeing chaos, we should see possibilities for God. Instead of languishing in our comfort zone, we should stand up and aggressively confront our situations. Instead of being sleeping giants, we should rise up and be counted, take our places in society, and claim God's promises.

Be Strategic: Use Weapons of Warfare

The old Scout motto, "Be prepared", has never been more relevant than today. We seek to create opportunities at the edge of chaos in a world where the devil has taken his stand to harass us in every way. One key strategy that God tells us to use is to be ready before we confront our enemy, to take the necessary precautions, and to deliberately arm ourselves with what the Bible calls "the whole armour of God".

The assumption here is that we make it our daily habit to train ourselves in the art of combat, using our weapons during our match practice. Just like any trainer who frequents the gym or is on the road daily, it becomes second nature when we are called upon to run the real race in a competition.

These weapons are not used on the day of battle but are used in dummy runs whenever they are needed. Our challenge is to get used to employing them on a daily basis. Remember, when David was given Saul's armour, he felt uncomfortable because it was not suitable, and he had not used this type of armour before.

You must be proactive, for this is not a physical battle but a spiritual one. Paul says that "we are not fighting against human beings but against the wicked spiritual forces in the heavenly world, the rulers, authorities, and cosmic powers of this dark age" (Eph. 6: 12, GNT). He goes on in 2 Cor. 10: 4, "The weapons we use in our fight are not the world's weapons but God's powerful weapons, which we use to destroy strongholds" (GNT). God does the resourcing. We simply access the resources.

This is the nature of the God we worship. He must be worshipped in Spirit and truth. The power we are promised comes from the Holy Spirit. This means that we need to be ready, always – armed with the necessary tools to wrestle the enemy.

You remember Joshua's encounter with the "Commander of the Lord's Army" who had come to encourage him to take on the fight. Remember Daniel in the fiery furnace where the king saw not only three people but also "a fourth one" who was an angel of God taking care of his people in the fire.

Daniel was found praying when the danger of death was lurking at his door. His was a lifestyle of prayer. His was a deployment of God's tried and tested weaponry which even the Son of God used in the garden of Gethsemane.

So taking the whole armour of God means being ready to strategically deal with the challenges of life, having prepared for them as part of our walk with Jesus. As sojourners, we are always restless, knowing that this is not our final destination. We are therefore always on the lookout, alert and vigilant.

What are the characteristics we should foster as part of our preparation for the evil day? These are truth, righteousness, the readiness that comes from the gospel of peace, faith, salvation, the word of God, prayer in the Spirit, and a constant alertness to pray, especially for the saints.

Truth is who Jesus is: "I am the way, the truth, and the life. No one comes to the Father except through me" (John 14: 6). The one we are in confrontation with is called the father of lies. What a contrast. It is a battle between truth and falsehood. We worship "the only true God", so no wonder part of our arsenal is truth. John refers to him as "the only begotten of the Father, full of grace and truth" (John 1: 14, NKJV).

What a contrast to the world we are living in, where we have tended to fight falsehood with falsehood. Truth has so been diluted that we can today ask, as Pilate asked Jesus, "What is truth?" Many people who tell the truth are a minority. Many have died for the truth when they could have easily told a lie and survived. Fighting against principalities and powers demands that we, like Jesus, tell the truth. When Satan tempted Jesus, he came up with a distorted view of the word of God in an attempt to lure Jesus from his mission. Jesus told the truth from the Word, and he stood his ground and won.

The challenge of today is for men and women to employ this tool for the glory of God. What a difference this will make to a world bent on survival tactics for now, devoid of any cost. That is why Peter said that if you are persecuted for the sake of Christ, you must count it a privilege, for you are doing what God wants.

If we are going to be prepared to use this tool, we must be in the habit of telling the truth always, at home, at work, and under any circumstance. There is need to repent in this area, as we sometimes find ourselves lacking the strength to be truthful. If we are going to do battle with the Father of lies on this front, we should be telling the truth, or else there will be no difference between ourselves and the enemy we are fighting against.

You prepare before the attack. You anticipate risk. You build this into your strategic plan for the crises ahead, so that even when you are at the edge of chaos, you know what to do and when and how to do it. There are no surprises!

Your Crisis Is Not a Setback but a Setup

What you regard as a setback in your life might be God's deliberately setting you up for something bigger and impactful. When Joni Eareckson was crippled in childhood, it never dawned on her parents that she would influence the world through her music and books. When people gang up against you to remove you from your workplace, they never realize that God has prepared a better job for you. When David was pursued by his enemies, even then God prepared a table in front of them.

Crisis? What crisis? It is a dangerous opportunity to serve God, to be the best CEO, the best gardener, the best wife, the best that can be. Joseph became a prince. Daniel was the governor. Esther became a queen who saved a nation.

Indeed opportunities can be created at the edge of chaos. Paul testified to this. "I can do all things through Christ who strengthens me" (Phil. 4: 13, NKJV) – all things, regardless of the situation or circumstance.

Examine your situation. How can you turn the setback into an opportunity?

Your Weakness Is Your Witness

Look beyond the crisis. Don't allow your weakness to affect your witness. Satan targets your Achilles heel. He reminds you that you are vulnerable. He glories in seeing your confidence diminish. He is the great reminder of your past.

Use your weakness to declare God's faithfulness in the past. Make a statement of God's goodness through your weakness.

David turned his dire moment of weakness with Bathsheba into the greatest confession psalm in history. He ended up pleading with God to bring back the joy of salvation. He asked God to create in him a new heart.

Many of us succumb to sin. When we fall into sin, we remain there and never get up. God is in the business of picking up the pieces. However depressed, run down, and defeated we may be, God can still transform that into something good.

We make the mistake of denigrating leaders who fall away. We become judgmental. We write them off. Not God! His love is at the ready to save the repentant sinner. He did it with David, Paul, the Prodigal Son, the woman caught in adultery, and many others.

All we have is the grace of God. It is not of our own doing. It remains God's prerogative.

Paul declared that he was the chief of sinners. And he went on, "by the grace of God I am what I am" (1 Cor. 15: 10, NIV). You are weak, but God is strong. He chose the foolish things of the world to shame the wise of this world. It is a contradiction. He raises the poor from the dust and makes them sit with princes. Who says you are weak? God says you are strong. He will nurture you and coach you. When you fall, you will rise again. Wow!

Knowledge Is Power

Jesus, in talking to the Pharisees, perceived why they were ineffective as leaders. They knew neither the Scriptures nor the power of God. They had neglected the manual of life, in many cases misinterpreting it to suit themselves.

You need to know what God's manual says. Knowing the Scriptures enables people to interpret history correctly and read the signs of the times, like the sons of Issachar (1 Chronicles 12:32) . Knowing the Scriptures gives the ability to address current situations using the appropriately prescribed tools.

In Hos. 4: 10 God says, "My people are destroyed for lack of knowledge." This has been the problem with many Christians today: not knowing what God says about a given situation. In Hebrews the Word of God is said to be sharper than a two-edged sword. In Ephesians, Paul describes it as the sword of the Spirit. Knowledge of what God says and what he can do through his word is a deterrent against any form of attack that may likely come against us. David says, "Your word is a lamp to guide me and a light for my path" (Ps. 119: 105, GNT). It has the sole purpose of helping us see where we are going, how we will get there, and the obstacles along the way.

This is what is meant by "the steps of the righteous are guided by the Lord". You can only interpret what is happening through a close study and understanding of God's Word. The problem with the Pharisees was that they were blind to what the Scriptures said and were only concerned with their own interpretations. The Scriptures are part of our weaponry to ward off the attacks of the evil one as well as a road map to help us chart the way forward on our journey.

When Jesus was tempted by the devil, he demonstrated his knowledge of the Scriptures and readily used them to withstand the temptations. He spoke the Word to counter the devil's falsehoods. We need to ask God to reveal to us the relevant Scriptures for a given situation. This is why a combination of the knowledge of the Scriptures and the power of God is necessary. Remember, Jesus was full of the Holy Spirit when he went into the desert and at the same time armed with knowledge of the Scriptures. This lethal combination ensures our survival in a world bereft of these two necessary ingredients.

Jesus criticized the Pharisees for being able to interpret the weather but not able to read the signs of the times like the people of Issachar (1 Chronicles 12:32). The sons of Issachar were diligent and careful to interpret the times they were living in.

The men of Berea were not content with just reading the Scriptures; they went a step further and examined everything they were taught. In other words, they were students of the Word and not merely passive recipients of it. They, like David, meditated upon it day and night. And the result was that they stayed well informed and were able to respond to their challenges in accordance with what the Word of God said. You cannot do this if the Scriptures are merely some sort of novel you go through without serious reflection on the implications of the message. One has to hear God's voice as one goes through the text. And this is possible only through seeking the Holy Spirit to reveal his Word to you.

You can create opportunities at the edge of chaos when you regard the Scriptures as your basic guide, when such knowledge informs your decisions, reactions, attitudes, and perceptions. Your mindset has to be resourced by what the Scriptures say. It has to be a paradigm shift, from self-determination of one's course of action to a Scripture-determined course of action.

Remember, Jesus from the word go was influenced by what the Scriptures had said about him. In fact, he was above all fulfilling God's purpose for his life on this earth. On many occasions in the Gospels there is a statement that events occurred to fulfil what the Scriptures had said.

Such a paradigm shift does not mean that we become robots,

incapable of thinking or taking appropriate action outside Scripture. What it does mean is that the source of our passion, competencies, and skills is in what the Scriptures say. We are strategic, wise, and persevering, just as the heroes of the faith were; creative and innovative, just as God was from the beginning; and serving, just as Jesus did. Remember, servant leadership is what drove Jesus to rescue us from oppression. All the characteristics of good and successful leadership have their origin in the Scriptures.

The Pharisees knew not the power of God. Lack of power from God through the Holy Spirit renders us useless for effective service. The person of the Holy Spirit is essential for service. At creation the Spirit was hovering over the waters, ready to empower creation for service. In the Old Testament, only those on whom the Spirit descended were able to do extraordinary work for God – for example, Samson, David, Elijah, and Elisha.

Jesus promised his disciples power and asked them not to leave Jerusalem until they had received the Spirit. He said, "When the Holy Spirit comes upon you, you will be filled with power, and you will be witnesses for me in Jerusalem, Judea, Samaria, and to the ends of the earth (Acts 1: 8).

We need to be strategic in our walk with Jesus and as we wrestle with the many challenges at home, in our workplace, and elsewhere. The Holy Spirit's power becomes strategic in that he enables us to be prepared for battle. We become proactive, always ready to face situations. Some of the functions of the Spirit include empowerment, recalling for us the words of Jesus, comfort, intercession (helping us pray), communication, and sustenance. With the Spirit we are able to speak God's word with power, enabling people to come to the knowledge of Jesus Christ.

The religious leaders had a problem. They lacked the authority and power that Jesus had; hence they were ineffective. They were unable to interpret the Word, as this, too, required the power of God.

This crucial issue faces many leaders in the church today.

Following Jesus has become a ritual. As Paul puts it, "They will hold to the outward form of our religion, but reject its real power" (2 Tim. 3: 5, GNT). Paul exhorts us to avoid such people. When Jesus chose the first disciples, he gave them power to drive out demons and to heal the sick. So God's presence through his Spirit was a sign that he was in operation. This is why it is not possible for us to create opportunities at the edge of chaos without the Spirit's enabling. This will help us remain focused on the task at hand and give us access to the inexhaustible resources at the Holy Spirit's disposal.

Knowing the power of God means being able to access the enabling strength to do business for God. It is the Spirit who prepares us, enables us, and sees us through the challenges of life – at work, at home, wherever.

Pick Up the Pieces

God is in the business of picking up the pieces. So are you. God is the potter. We are the clay. You have been broken. Leaders have been broken.

Pastors and leaders do mess up. They are caught in adultery or lying; they embezzle funds or just suffer a broken heart, feeling polluted. God mends. He restores. David in the Bible messed up big-time, but God forgave him and restored him.

If God does this, all the time, what about you? Creating opportunities at the edge of chaos means picking up those who have let you and themselves down, those who have not lived up to the standard.

The woman caught in adultery was told by Jesus, "Sin no more." He embraced her, not condoning what she had done but urging her to live life differently.

Don't Forget

It all starts with who we are in Christ and what he has done for us. The deliverance of the people of Israel from Egypt on the night the angel "passed over" the houses of the Israelites and spared them from destruction was the first pointer to our deliverance by the "Passover Lamb", who is Jesus. We were spared from destruction by the blood of Jesus that was shed on the cross.

We need to be reminded again and again of such a rich heritage. Our guarantee of not only meeting Jesus in heaven but experiencing the release of power to live our lives today in the anointing that comes from Christ. Through the Holy Communion we are asked to remember Jesus until he comes again. Through Jesus, salvation's wondrous plan was wrought. We are redeemed, we were bought with a price. We are heirs, we are priceless, we are God's masterpieces. And if we are all this, we can live in expectancy, hope, and courage, for we know we are not on our own.

The liberation of the nation of Israel on the day the angel passed over their houses marks the beginning of God's untangling the chains that had bound his people. And thousands of years later Jesus came to free us from sin and restore us to our original position of freedom. Jesus says in John, "So if the Son sets you free, you will be free indeed" (John 8: 36). We start from a position of freedom.

This is our status. Our attitude to what is happening around us is interpreted in accordance with the mindset of freedom that Christ gives us. This means that our reaction to events around us can never be gloomy and pessimistic. Why? Because we are children of hope and not of despair. We worship and follow a living Saviour, not a dead one. We dare hope because we embrace a Saviour whose very nature is hope. We have faith because he has faith. We rejoice because he rejoices. We persevere because he persevered.

I was touched when preparing a sermon on the Holy

Communion to realize how important it is for us to always remember the history of our great salvation. We do this in remembrance of Jesus. It is a reminder of where we are coming from, what God has done for us, and how costly it was for us to be bought back by Jesus.

This realization regularly will enable us to continue to withstand the struggles of life that we face each day. We will experience a new vigour, a new spirit, which will propel us to go forward in hope and faith. In the words of an old chorus, "Love lifted me, love lifted me. When nothing else could help, love lifted me" (Alan Jackson). His love did it for us. While we were yet sinners, Christ died for us.

We were forgiven. We were bought with a price. Can you imagine what went through Zacchaeus's mind when Jesus said to him that salvation had come to his house? This was after all he had done wrong, extorting other people's property over the years. And yet here was the King of Kings, the Saviour of the world, putting into operation what God had promised thousands of years ago: redemption for humankind. The Lamb of God was now effecting the plan of God predestined from the beginning of history. Here was the restoration of a wayward person instantly through the power of Jesus.

When John the Baptist, remarked, "There is the Lamb of God who takes away the sin of the world" (John 1: 29), he was testifying to the fulfilment of the history of humankind's salvation. For John, Jesus was the archetype of the Passover lamb without which we would have no hope for our salvation.

During the Passover the people of God were spared from destruction because the angel found the blood of the lamb sprinkled on their doorposts. In the same manner we are spared from eternal damnation when we embrace the blood of Jesus and allow him to sprinkle us with his blood. Now, when God looks at us, he no longer sees our sin but Jesus's blood. And because we have this guarantee through the blood, we can approach God's throne with boldness. What confidence! So lest we forget, our track record is the history of our great salvation.

No wonder we can create opportunities at the edge of chaos, because we are confident that he who began a good work in us will see it to fruition.

We are aware that when God created the heavens and the earth, there was nothing. Out of the void, darkness, and vast water mass, God was able to speak order into the universe. Choice is a precursor of order and opportunity.

For Jesus, no one is utterly useless. He came to seek and to serve the lost. Whoever believes in him will not perish but have everlasting life. In God's world there is no one who can be termed a "write-off"; all of us have the potential to be reconstituted and made whole again through the power of Jesus.

We live in a world where people get fed up with others and decide to condemn them. This has never been the character of our God. When David sinned against God, he confessed before the prophet Nathan, who immediately told David that God had forgiven him. What happened next is the greatest story ever told of someone whom God loves until the end. When the woman caught in adultery was paraded before Jesus by so-called religious leaders, Jesus turned it into an object lesson on forgiveness. None of the leaders could stay behind when Jesus asked those without sin to remain behind.

We all taken from the scrap heap and made into masterpieces through the blood of the Lamb. This realization of what he has done for us does not end here. It is our launch pad as we walk in faith to meet the Saviour in heaven. There is an expectancy that keeps us on our toes, prompts us to live in expectation, and drives us to live for Jesus each day. This is a desire to do much more for him as the Day draws near.

It is a mindset that insists we are more than conquerors. This is what inspired Stephen in the face of death. This is what should inspire you. What a hope, what tenacity against all odds. But remember, Stephen as a deacon was filled with the Holy Spirit, wisdom, and faith. He knew where he was going, his destiny and the fulfilment of God's great salvation. Chaos? What chaos? When the Lamb is with us, when we understand the history of our great salvation, we can stand tall and proclaim, "He lives, He lives, Christ Jesus lives today. He walks with me and he talks with me along life's narrow way. You ask me how I know he lives; he lives within my heart" (Alfred Ackley).

We need to bear in mind what God has done for us through Jesus. He has been in the business of reconstruction from time immemorial. He created the world out of nothing. Before creation, we are told, the earth was without form and void, a vast expanse of waters with nothing except the Spirit hovering over the face of the deep. And when God said, "Let there be light", there was light, and that was the beginning of form and organization and the rest of creation as we know it today.

When humanity sinned through Adam, God decided to execute his plan of salvation through the blood, first of goats and other animals and finally through the Lamb. Knowledge of what God has done for us inspires us to live this life and the next with great humility, faith, passion, and confidence.

Be Authentic

We may become accomplished in growing counterfeit fruit – fruit that looks good on the shelf but won't be Christ's genuine, lasting, healthy fruit.

Authentic leaders are vulnerable. They don't pretend. They live in accordance with their moral absolutes. They risk without risking their reputation. They care about genuineness and care less about what others think. They go into chaotic situations seeking opportunities, nothing more and nothing less.

Jesus was an example of authenticity. He was open, transparent. He was fearless. "You hypocrites!" he called some of the eminent religious leaders. He was seen using a whip to drive entrepreneurs from the temple! Authentic leaders are zealous, passionate, and vision-driven.

Paul was authentic. He was the real deal. What you saw was what you got. His experience of Jesus was life-changing. Nothing could sidetrack him from it. "For me to live is Christ, and to die is gain", he wrote from prison (Phil. 1: 21). "We are more than conquerors", he reminded the people of Rome who were under persecution (Rom. 8: 37).

Circumstances never change one's authenticity. Peer pressure doesn't either. Do you measure up to this authenticity test? Authentic leaders have a track record. Their CV emboldens their cause.

When King Hezekiah was told he was going to die, he challenged God. "Look at my track record," he said. And God rescinded his decision. He was given another fifteen years! His record was a bargaining chip. Paul wrote, "Be imitators of me as I am of Christ" (1 Cor. 11: 1). Authentic leaders lead by example. Their lives are an open template, a letter to be read by all. They have nothing to hide. What a difference from many in leadership today. Concealed in their ethical cupboards are strange and unsavoury things, scandals galore. They are like the blind leading the blind.

Be Truthful

You cannot fake who you are. This was Jesus's characteristic. He came full of grace and truth. His reputation remained intact. Even his enemies acknowledged this. One of the Roman centurions confessed that he was the Son of God.

Do people acknowledge you as the real deal? I mean your children, peers, workmates, and colleagues. Daniel, a foreigner in the high echelons of power in Babylon demonstrated this. "They could find no corruption in him for he was trustworthy ..."(Daniel 6:4). This is the ultimate test, the true standard: real character.

More and more corporate organizations are realizing the need for this ethical bar to be set higher than before. It is no longer business as usual. Everything is under scrutiny. A culture of ethical excellence is now well sought after. You cannot put a price on honesty and integrity. They have become the bedrock of what leadership par excellence means.

Be daring. When you are authentic, the one who dares wins! This is not a blind faith. It is an informed faith, boldly seizing opportunities, knowing that some windows of opportunity never open up again.

Many years ago, I was offered three tracts of land for a song. Granted, I had just bought a house and was unable to raise the capital. Still this was an opportunity of a lifetime. Today the same tracts of land are worth thousands of dollars. The opportunity was there, but it was lost, and I can only cry over spilt milk.

For you it may be an opportunity to talk to someone about the saving power of Christ. You wish you had done so. But the person is tragically killed in an accident. A missed opportunity.

Zacchaeus, a revenue and customs official, climbed a tree to see Jesus. He got his reward. He was never the same again. Salvation had come to his house. He was eternally transformed.

People talk of lost opportunities, but the good news is, more opportunities come our way. Be on the lookout! Be vigilant, be prepared, be strategic – and go for it.

Being authentic sometimes entails acknowledging our flawed self, the dark self, the mask we sometimes wear to protect our fragile self . We need to "acknowledge and come to terms with the darker side of our nature, the warrior, the killer, the aggressor, the calculator, the manipulator, the thief, the exploiter - in one word, our vices." Robert J. Starrat 2003

Do Good to Everyone

Many of the opportunities that God gives us are for a purpose: to do good. This means that we don't have many options except to do good, to be sure we make a difference in people's lives. And if you examine the life of Christ on this earth, you see that his passion was to do good to everyone he met: the woman with the issue of blood, the woman with a bent back for the last eighteen years, Jairus's twelve-year-old daughter, Simon Peter's mother-in-law. There was never a time when Jesus came in contact with anyone and did not do good. Even when he met his enemies, his desire was not for their destruction but for their salvation. Zacchaeus, a tax collector, encountered the goodness of God when Jesus said, "Come down, for I must stay at your house today" (Luke 19: 5). We might have seen only a man in a tree; Jesus noticed an opportunity to do good.

And the doing of good is to everyone. Paul in Galatians 6 qualifies this by saying "particularly to those of the faith". So as we encounter those who believe as we do, we should desire to do more good. What a contrast to what we sometimes do when we don't tolerate others and seek to discriminate or separate ourselves from them. It is always good from time to time to check our record as to how much good we have done to others in the course of a given day, week, or month. Record the events, and see what happened. See how you can improve on this record.

Rather than expecting people to do good to you, go for it, and do good to other people. This will bless you and inspire you to do more. In fact, your self-image will improve, and you will find more purpose to be on this planet! Living for |Jesus will take on a new dimension.

Become a Shepherd

Be selfless. Care for others. Create opportunities for others even at the edge of chaos. Ezekiel makes this observation:

> Son of man, prophesy against the shepherds of Israel; prophesy, and say to them, even to the shepherds, Thus says the Lord GOD: Ah, shepherds of Israel who have been feeding yourselves! Should not shepherds feed the sheep? You eat the fat, you clothe yourselves with the wool, you slaughter the fat ones, but you do not feed the sheep. The weak you have not strengthened, the sick you have not healed, the injured you have not bound up, the strayed you have not brought back, the lost you have not sought, and with force and harshness you have ruled them. So they were scattered, because there was no shepherd, and they became food for all the wild beasts. My sheep were scattered; they wandered over all the mountains and on every high hill. My sheep were scattered over all the face of the earth, with none to search or seek for them. (Ezek. 34: 2–6)

Peter illustrates graphically the concept of leadership by introducing the leader as the overseer, a shepherd of the sheep. Shepherding is overseeing God's work on behalf of the great Shepherd who will ultimately reward those who would have done the work of shepherding on his behalf.

Notice that 1 Peter 5:2-3, outlines the key functions of the shepherd, the overseer, who does his work willingly. There is no compulsion. You serve as in response to God's call. This is why it is important to lead where your heart is. This will bring joy and passion to whatever you do. It will also affect your attitude towards those you seek to serve.

Our desire as leaders is to influence others to achieve the goals and objectives of our ministry or organization. Eagerness implies zeal, passion, and commitment, a dogged determination to succeed, whatever the odds against us. Those who are eager derive some inspiration from the task at hand. They demonstrate an inner strength that keeps them going on and on, setting an example as they go.

We are to be *role models*. An elder was someone who was mature, dignified, and a good example in the community. This is where the concept of *servant leadership* comes from. They are authentic, not fake, and their lives reflect their character. They are people of *integrity*.

Be Mature

Mature people are sober minded. They are not tossed to and fro by every wind of doctrine. They stick to the plan. They depend on what God says. They remain focused, dependable, and resolute. When you are at the edge, you surely need maturity, but it has become a rare commodity, even among leaders and parents.

Paul says this about maturity

> So Christ himself gave the apostles, the prophets, the evangelists, the pastors and teachers, to equip his people for works of service, so that the body of Christ may be built up until we all reach unity in the faith and in the knowledge of the Son of God and become mature, attaining to the whole measure of the fullness of Christ.
>
> Then we will no longer be infants, tossed back and forth by the waves, and blown here and there by every wind of teaching and by the cunning and craftiness of people in their deceitful scheming. (Eph. 4: 11–14, NIV 2011)

Immature leaders react. That produces a lot of energy, but the problem is that it's toxic fuel. Mature leaders are proactive. They prevent fires rather than fighting them. You are in it for the long haul. You have staying power. Are you mature? You can be. Begin the process.

Resist the Temptation

Leaders need to guard against abuse of power and privilege. "Within each of us there is a herd of wild horses all waiting to run loose" (Wallace Hamilton) – the problem of the inner conflict, the *me* that I think I am raising its ugly head.

"Jesus knew when to refuse the cocktail of privilege, fame and applause that distorts one's ability to think wisely and to master himself" (*Leadership Today*, Gordon MacDonald, 2006).

The secret of leadership is to realize that we are all vulnerable. We need to make ourselves vulnerable to the Spirit in order to redeem our ego. This means leading from a tender place where I do not have all the answers.

"What makes the temptation of power so seemingly irresistible is that power offers an easy substitute for the hard task of love" (Henri Nouwen). This is a great challenge. Nations have risen or fallen on this. Leaders have succumbed to this, which is one of the three G's of leadership: gold, girls, and glory. Jesus overcame this temptation in the wilderness when Satan promised him kingdoms if only he could worship him. Like Jesus, don't. Only God must be worshipped.

Be Competent

God gives the skills. They are wrapped in wisdom – Holy Spirit skills. When the people of Israel started building the tabernacle there was no shortage of skills.

Know what you are good at. Do it with all your heart. Competence means skills for the tasks required. Doors open when you have skills. Sharpen your skills before opportunities come your way. If you are not competent, find someone else.

Win Over Worry

not knowing what tomorrow will bring has been a source of distraction for many of us.

How we wish we could control both today and tomorrow. Remember the children of Israel in the wilderness of the Sinai desert? When they complained over the lack of meat, God promised them manna. And the rules for consuming this latest version of wilderness beef was that you had to eat one portion per day, on the day as allocated. You could not carry over the next day what was meant for that day. In other words, God was saying enjoy today, and leave tomorrow to take care of itself. Only be assured that the portion for tomorrow will definitely be there for you.

How well this fits in with the prayer that Jesus taught his disciples: "Give us this day our daily bread." Or his advice to the disciples in the Sermon on the Mount: "Let tomorrow take care of itself." Contentment means being satisfied with the provisions of the day and having faith for the provisions of tomorrow. This is not "by chance planning"; this is strategic planning, out of a sense of conviction that he who has provided for the day and allowed me to enjoy it will do so tomorrow, as there is no reason to doubt such provision.

Being distracted, by what has not been and what we have not seen, tends to derail our plans and energy for the day at hand. We live in a psychological limbo, unable to fulfil our desires and ambitions. We tend to postpone until tomorrow what may be for today. Jesus lived for today. He realized that in order to achieve his mission, he had to work daily and not worry about what tomorrow might bring.

Do you realize that many of the things we worry about never happen as we fear they will? Worry essentially means distraction, when we lose focus. Focus on the important things of life. If you are idle or have "nothing to do", the tendency is for the mind to wander off and entertain other negative thoughts. Jesus knew this about his disciples, so he told them, "Seek ye first the kingdom of God and his righteousness, and all these things shall be added unto you" (Matt. 6: 33, KJV).

Focus on what God wants for your life, those things that will make you into a better person that pleases God. Once your energy and passion are directed that way, you minimize your possibility of losing direction. In any case, Jesus said, "I am the way, and the truth, and the life. No one comes to the Father except through me" (John 14: 6).

Be Careful What You Call Impossible!

The world is teetering on the edge, every day – morally, socially, economically. You have to survive. You need the competencies to do so. You cannot remain in the comfort zone.

There is no comfort zone. You are called upon to take the challenge. Jesus lived on the edge. So should we. And the angel who went to visit the ageing Sarah, wife of Abraham summed it up. "Is anything too hard for the Lord?" That is the mindset at the edge of chaos. Nothing is impossible. Opportunities abound, if you look for them.

It is hard work. It requires persistence, perseverance, and tenacity. There is a price to pay. Are you willing to pay that price? Go on then. Create opportunities at the edge of chaos – in this world – today!